Also by Tessa Bridal

Fiction

The Tree of Red Stars

River of Painted Birds
Available in Spanish as: Río de los pájaros pintados

Nonfiction

Exploring Museum Theatre

Effective Exhibit Interpretation and Design

ISBN: 978-1-73693860-7 (Paperback)
ISBN: 978-1-73693861-4 (eBook)
Library of Congress Control Number: 2021915817
Invisble Ink

Illustration by Sylvia Crannell. Cover photo by Javier Noceti.

Praise for *The Tree of Red Stars*

"Tessa Bridal brings a fresh voice to Latin American literature in her first novel, *The Tree of Red Stars*. Bridal, who was born and raised in Uruguay, uses her book to present a harrowing account of that country's takeover by a military dictatorship, a regime that violently demolished one of Latin America's oldest democracies. As the story leads up to these dramatic events, Bridal describes life in Montevideo through the eyes of Magda, a young woman from an upper-middle-class family who has lived a sheltered and secure existence - until the growing political unrest threatens to erupt even within her own wealthy neighborhood. And when Magda's friends and their families are endangered, she is forced to make use of her privileges in ways that will also be hazardous to herself. Bridal's narrative concentrates on a matter-of-fact rendering of Magda's transformation into a revolutionary, dispelling stereotypical notions about the relationship between social class and volatile political activism. Magda's association with the socialist Tupamaro guerrillas stems less from entrenched political beliefs than from her loyalty to her friends and her love for the country in which she has spent her childhood. As *The Tree of Red Stars* proceeds, Bridal recounts Magda's perilous activities with a chillingly understated sense of inevitability."

— *THE NEW YORK TIMES BOOK REVIEW*

" . . . Set in 1960's Uruguay, Tessa Bridal's first novel - winner of this year's (1997) Milkweed National Fiction Prize - is a skillful, utterly engrossing portrait of a social conscience awakening against fervent and often furtive friendships, personal and political loyalty, filial defiance and impossible love. . . . *The Tree of Red Stars* is an unpredictable and exquisite story."

Praise for *The Dark Side of Memory*

"A bright star in a constellation of creative nonfiction works about the violent conflicts of mid-late 20th century in Latin America, the book casts a profound human gaze on a most devastating personal and social tragedy. *The Dark Side of Memory* weaves its narrative slowly. It pulls you in until you are compelled to read on in spite of a growing sense of foreboding. You are entering the sacred grounds of deep loss and deaths foretold, only, you are doing so held by Bridal's compassionate hand and beautifully evocative voice. It lifts the lesser known stories of Uruguayan victims of the dictatorships that plagued South America's "southern cone" up to the altar of quotidian, anonymous heroism where they belong. Critically, it centers its narrative on the behind-the-scenes epic struggle to recover defenseless young children, some born in clandestine torture centers where their mothers were murdered by those who kept them as their own. In doing so, Bridal offers us a poignant, clear-eyed view of the conflict, to best measure the viciousness of the military's actions, and the courageous resilience of survivors and relatives who never gave up on their abducted kin. In the age of Black Lives Matter and the brutal detention of children by US Immigration Enforcement at the border, *The Dark Side of Memory* is a most caring and powerful cautionary tale as to the enduring, generational nature of trauma when political violence is unleashed on those most vulnerable."

— *ROBERTO GUTIÉRREZ VAREA, DIRECTOR, LATIN AMERICAN STUDIES PROGRAM, UNIVERSITY OF SAN FRANCISCO*

"Tessa Bridal's *The Dark Side of Memory* has the immediacy of a novel. We travel alongside a group of indefatigable women: into the torture centers of the Argentine military junta; through their long bureaucratic battles to rescue the children who were stolen from them. This is a book about the way the violence of the past weighs on the future, shaping its possibilities. And it is also a book about how acknowledging that past—fighting against the seductions of forgetting—opens a less violent, more human future."

— *TOBY ALTMAN, NATIONAL ENDOWMENT FOR THE ARTS 2021-2022 FELLOW IN POETRY*

"This is a holy book—because it tells the truth, concretely and unflinchingly. In the midst of an inferno, *The Dark Side of Memory* points us to the lives of the mothers and grandmothers of Uruguay and Argentina who, out of great love for their children, refused to permit the perpetrators of devastation to have the final word. Tessa Bridal bears witness to the power of memory, truth-telling, and hope, and so also to the possibility of a just world. This is a tremendous work of love."

— *RY O. SIGGELKOW, DIRECTOR OF INITIATIVES IN FAITH & PRAXIS, UNIVERSITY OF ST. THOMAS IN ST. PAUL, MN*

"These life stories, portrayed in all their vivid complexity by Tessa Bridal, honor the humanity of the many who were dehumanized by Latin America's dirty wars. Her creative telling brings us as close as we can get to grasping the motivations behind the crime of enforced disappearance, and to feeling for ourselves its deep and lasting scars upon victims, families and societies."

— *BARBARA FREY, DIRECTOR, HUMAN RIGHTS PROGRAM, UNIVERSITY OF MINNESOTA*

THE DARK SIDE OF MEMORY

Uruguay's Disappeared Children
and the Families
That Never Stopped Searching

TESSA BRIDAL

To my daughters Anna and Kate with abiding love and admiration.

AUTHOR'S NOTE

The historical events in this book are all true.

The word "disappeared" is used to describe adults and children illegally captured and/or kidnapped by military and paramilitary forces during the Cold War years (post World War II to early 1990's). No official record of them existed, and families have spent years, and in some cases decades, searching for them.

* * *

The book focuses on four implacable and tenacious women determined to find their disappeared children and grandchildren, even when searching for them endangered their own lives and freedom.

The men behind the disappearances documented here were part of an international web involved not only in trafficking minors, but in assassinations that took place from Washington DC to Rome, Paris and Buenos Aires.

In this book, to make the politics, history, people and personal stories more accessible to readers, who might be unfamiliar with the culture and complex history of the times, I include dialogue based on firsthand testimonies and reliable sources. When documentary sources were credible but couldn't be entirely verified, I have taken literary license.

A note on names: in Latin American countries, children are given two first names. Unlike the U.S. where the second name often becomes an initial and rarely forms part of a person's everyday name, in Latin American countries both names are often used;

a person is known as María Julia or Juan Alberto. At other times, the first or second name is dropped in everyday usage. Women commonly retain their surnames when they marry, and children are given both the father and mother's paternal names. So in most cases, children will have two first names and two surnames. As in many cultures, names are often abbreviated. For example, Emilia, one of the disappeared mothers, is often called Emi by her relatives and friends.

Any errors or misinterpretations are mine.

DRAMATIS PERSONAE

Sara Méndez
Mauricio, Simón's father
Simón, their son
Gerardo, Mauricio's brother

Maria Ester Gatti de Islas
Emilia, her daughter
Jorge, Emilia's husband
Mariana Zaffaroni Islas

Amaral
Yolanda, his mother
Floreal, his father
Maricel, Floreal's sister, Amaral's aunt
Alberto, Maricel's husband, Amaral's uncle

Blanca Artigas
Mary, her daughter – María
Asunción Artigas Nilo de
Moyano
Fredi, Mary's husband
Victoria, Mary and Fredi's
daughter

Elena and **Antonio**
Andrés and **Gabriel**, their
nephews
Violeta Velasco, Antonio's
mother
Ramón, Antonio's father
and Jorge's daughter
Carla, Mercedes, Josefina,
Antonio's sisters
Alejandro, Antonio's brother
Fernando, Carla's husband
Sergio Reyes, Josefina's fiancée

13

INTRODUCTION

May 2000

A s deep and as wide as the sorrow its people have endured is the river that separates Buenos Aires from its small neighbor, Montevideo.

As the plane banked preparatory to its descent into Montevideo Airport, I saw the Río de la Plata below me and remembered how during the summer months of December, January, and February, thousands of Argentines would leave their sprawling capital and cross the Río de la Plata to bask on the golden sands of Uruguay's beaches. In spite of the disdain with which we often speak of one another, Uruguayans and Argentines are closely bound by language, culture, friends, and family. Citizens of our two countries inter-marry, schools compete at sporting events, and people address one another by the informal, friendly *¡che!*

I looked down at the green landscape, half expecting that it, like Uruguay itself, would have undergone a dramatic change during my decade-long absence. But the rivers and streams still ran between farms; sheep and cattle grazed on the plains; and the seemingly endless Río de la Plata merged with the Atlantic Ocean, gifting Uruguay's eastern coast with a golden ribbon of sandy beaches.

Most of my childhood memories were associated with that river and those beaches. In winter we'd walked them with our dogs, in summer we'd bathed, in the sun and in the river, gathered in groups with friends to swim and play and plan weekend dances. We had danced for pleasure, for love, and during Carnival, for fun. Dancers would break out onto the streets in long *conga* lines and neighbors of all ages joined in, circling the light poles and trees, finally returning inside to eat potato chips and drink Coca Cola.

* * *

I was twenty years old when my family decided to immigrate to the United States. I cried from the moment we boarded the Pan American flight until we were well on our way to Washington DC, at which point I finally fell asleep.

I remember most poignantly the effort to adjust to what at the time felt like insurmountable cultural differences. Alcohol was freely consumed at parties where the lights were dim and where dancing seemed a prelude to sex. People did not 'air kiss' on the cheek when being introduced. Most had only two names—a first and a last name—and women changed their last names to their husbands' when they married.

As a means of mourning, of celebrating, and of escaping into the familiar, I began writing fictional stories, published later in two novels set in Uruguay.

Now I was returning to interview the families of four of the Uruguayan children who disappeared during the Cold War years, when Uruguay's democracy, one of the oldest in Latin America, fell to a military dictatorship, along with the democracies of Brazil, Argentina, Bolivia, Paraguay, Chile, Peru, Ecuador, Guatemala, Panama and Honduras. Resistance movements existed in all these countries, and each had a story to tell. I was focusing on my own country—Uruguay—and on Argentina, where most Uruguayans sought refuge after a military takeover of their own country. Not long afterwards, Argentina's democracy also fell, and Uruguayans there were arrested and began to disappear, often along with their children. While I was not among those arrested during these times, friends and members of my family were.

Democracy returned to Uruguay in 1985, a few years before I began my research. I was by then the mother of two daughters, and the plight of the mothers and grandmothers searching for their disappeared children and grandchildren touched me deeply. The more I learned about their courage and resilience, the more I respected and admired them. I wanted to meet them in person and invite them to tell me their stories.

Argentina was one of the last South American democracies to fall, and by the time it did, in 1976, thousands who had sought refuge there including several hundred Uruguayans, had already disappeared into the hands of paramilitary forces. The number continued to escalate for the remainder of the decade until it reached 9,000 (the official figure) or 35,000 (the unofficial figure). Most were adults, but it is estimated that between 1970 and 1976 approximately twenty Uruguayan children also went missing, in most cases along with their parents.

The number of those unaccounted for is imprecise, since it is unknown how many women were pregnant at the time they were taken to the secret detention centers, where many of them gave birth. Some of the children were subsequently found in orphanages, some had been adopted by families ignorant of the child's origins, and some were appropriated by families associated with the regimes that killed the parents. Seven of the children were murdered, and accusations have been made that many of those still unaccounted for were sold in Europe.

Some of the disappeared children were babies and recall nothing of the moments when they were separated from their parents. Others were toddlers or older and can often conjure graphic images and vivid feelings of their last moments with their families.

Some disappeared for days or weeks, others for years or decades. When the children were located living with families, decisions had to be made regarding if, when, and how to reveal their true identities to them. Their reactions ranged from rejection to acceptance of their situation and of the strangers so anxious to claim them as their own.

The stories of the survivors of this state-sponsored terror share similarities, but each is as unique as the person who related it.

When democracy finally returned to Uruguay in 1985, debates began regarding the release of political prisoners and amnesty for both them and for the military who had imprisoned them. The country had been through a decade of turmoil and people were anxious to get back to normal. This led to a period when many people wanted to put it all behind them and were unwilling to participate in movements demanding that the military be held accountable for their actions during the years they were in power.

This desire to move on can be partially explained in Uruguay by one of the country's favorite sayings: *"somos pocos y nos conocemos,"* which means "there are few of us and we know each another." It was a rare family that did not have a relative or friend involved on one side of the conflict or the other, and in some families, on both sides.

Perhaps an uncle had been a guerilla, or a friend aware that people were being tortured at military headquarters. The family doctor might have seen to wounded guerillas and their prisoners. Or perhaps he was one of those who turned a blind eye when called by the military to attend a victim of torture. Friends and work colleagues found themselves walking a precarious tightrope in order to maintain professional and personal relationships.

I was not at all sure how my return and my research would be received. Those of us who left Uruguay, especially for the United States, were not always looked upon favorably.

Thanks to a friend, artist María Ester Francia, who had been imprisoned for her political activities, and had given birth in prison, I was introduced to the organization *Familias de los detenidos desaparecidos* (Families of the Detained Disappeared). Introductions followed and the generosity I encountered was unbounded. Homes were opened to me, treasured photos, letters, and mementos were shared, and painful events revisited, always with the hope that if people knew and understood what had happened and why, the mistakes of the past would not be repeated.

* * *

Blanca Artigas left the little gate in her front garden unlatched and her front door open as a sign of welcome. As I walked down the steps and along the narrow path flanked by ferns and flowers, I noticed a large crack in the door lintel. Blanca explained that it had been made three decades before by Uruguayan Major José Nino Gavazzo and the men who arrested both of her sons, and later her daughter, Mary. At first, Blanca had left the crack un-mended, as a constant reminder, almost a mark of honor. As she aged and the crack widened, she would have liked to have it repaired, but by then she couldn't afford the expense.

We sat in her small front room, where twenty years before she had had a *quiosquito*—a tiny market where she sold sweets. The room now contained a well-worn sofa where Blanca spent nights, since the ceiling in her bedroom was disintegrating and pieces of it could land on her while she slept. A small television set sat in a corner by the fireplace, and a stack of kindling was piled by the hearth. The fireplace would be lit only after sunset when there would be no other way of warming the room. The table was covered with old photos, carefully wrapped in plastic to protect them from the damp. Most of them were of Mary, her dark, shoulder-length hair blowing behind her as she smiled for the camera; some are of Mary's husband Fredi; and many of their daughter Victoria, a small replica of her mother, with a naughty grin and freshly curled hair.

Wrapped in a woolen cardigan in the same shade of gray as her hair, Blanca sat on a dark brown sofa and I on a chair across from her. There is a quiet strength about her. She looks at me with interest as if trying to understand why I traveled from the United States to talk with her.

She starts by telling me that while she had not been much interested in politics and had devoted herself to her home, her husband had been a union activist. She mentions with pride that he was a descendant of Uruguay's greatest national hero—José Gervasio Artigas—and that some relatives of his still receive a pension from the government as a result.

Blanca herself never attended university, though her daughter Mary did, and Blanca smiled as she remembered how Mary used to love sharing her lessons with her. She was studying medicine, and often it was late when she returned from classes and from attending the political meetings that so worried Blanca. She would wait up for Mary, standing outside in her small garden ready to greet her.

"You give me courage, *mamá*," Mary would tell her mother. "I see you in the distance and I'm no longer afraid."

Mary loved children and did what she could for the poorest ones in their humble neighborhood. Blanca remembers a little boy who lived in a *ranchito* (a dwelling made of left-over building materials) who was a great favorite of her daughter's. "She would bring him here and give him a bath and wash his clothes. At night, before he left, she'd give him bread and a big glass of milk."

At twenty-two, Blanca tells me, Mary married a young Argentine called Fredi Moyano, and a week later, they left for Buenos Aires.

I tell Blanca that I have two daughters, and she asks to see photos of them. She is surprised that I have none with me and chides me. I tell her that she reminds me of my mother, who had recently died. She leans over and takes my hands in her two broad, strong ones.

"I am so sorry."

I thank her and say that while I mourn my mother deeply, I can't imagine how I would bear the loss of a daughter.

Blanca releases my hands and sits up very straight. "By fighting!" she says. "By never giving in!"

* * *

Ester Gatti de Islas no longer wanted to speak of the past.

Two decades of traipsing through the courts and facing the barriers of entrenched bureaucracies in her efforts to locate her daughter Emilia and son-in-law Jorge's bodies plus the fight to gain custody of her granddaughter Mariana had exhausted Ester. She personally confronted the Uruguayan officer operating in Argentina who took Mariana. She believes he was also responsible for Emilia and Jorge's disappearance: that same Major José Nino Gavazzo who left his mark on Blanca's house.

Ester chaired the Uruguayan national commission to repeal the amnesty granted to the military after democracy was reinstated. Before her loss weighed her down, she granted interviews to the media, always hoping that someone would heed her appeal and come forward with information about Mariana, and the whereabouts of Emilia and Jorge's bodies.

She left the story of her daughter Emilia (often called Emi by family and friends), her son-in-law Jorge, and her granddaughter Mariana for her friend and biographer Mariela Salaberry to share with me. Mariela's generosity was absolute. She granted me access to and permission to use the family stories and letters she collected in her interviews with Ester, compiled in a published report titled *Mariana, tú y nosotros* (Mariana, You and Us).

* * *

Elena and Antonio (not their real names) prefer to remain anonymous.

My meeting with them was arranged by a mutual friend and took place in her house. It would be the first time they shared their story outside of the family and a few friends.

They sat close together on a small sofa, an attractive couple in their late forties or early fifties. Elena, very slim and elegant, did most of the talking. It was clear that she had a lot to say about the ordeal they had gone through. Antonio supported her and added bits of humor to their narrative.

When their first child was one-and-a-half years old and they were expecting their second, Antonio's sister Carla and her husband Fernando were arrested in Buenos Aires. Carla and Fernando's one-and-a-half-year-old baby and his one-month-old brother were handed over to neighbors, who in turn gave them to the police, who later denied any knowledge of them.

The children were eventually found in an orphanage in Buenos Aires and smuggled into Elena and Antonio's home in Montevideo. The one-year-old, Gabriel, held his head up, with a hard look, as if nothing could touch him. His baby brother had lost his suction reflex and was not expected to live.

For nearly three decades after the children's rescue little reference was made to how they came to be in the orphanage, or to how they were found and brought to Uruguay. Elena and Antonio were surprised when, after they agreed to tell me the part they played in the rescue, they found out that Gabriel wanted to be interviewed as well.

Gabriel, now an adult, was eager to share his memories, and received me in his neat little house. His look was direct and his head held high. A dark, handsome, and athletic young man, his movements were brisk as he made *mate*˙ tea. A lace cloth covered the table in the front room and a plate of heart shaped cookies awaited me. I put the pastries I had brought next to the plate of cookies and suddenly we burst out laughing at the idea of talking for so long that we would actually consume all the food before us.

It was a chilly autumn day and Gabriel noticed that I was feeling the cold. He moved the electric heater closer and asked politely if I would mind if he let the dog in. I told him that I would like to meet his pet and the feeling turned out to be mutual. Carbón was extremely large, with the head of a Rottweiler and the supple body of a Labrador Retriever. He would have sat in my lap had his size made that possible but had to be content with lying on my feet by the heater while Gabriel and I sipped our *mate*.*

I made a start by helping myself to one of the heart-shaped cookies, and Gabriel leaned back with the *mate* gourd in his hand.

He tells me that his recollections of his early years of childhood aren't very clear and memories of his mother few. He lived with his aunt and uncle, Elena and Antonio, and their two children. His first memory of his mother is of seeing her through a set of bars in the visiting room of her prison near Buenos Aires. He and his brother made the journey with his aunt and uncle from Montevideo to Buenos Aires by boat, and he recalls looking down at the water going by, thinking how big everything was. He was two or three.

"This is your mother," someone said when they arrived at the prison. He was asked to kiss her, and he put his head through the

---

* Mate is a green tea enjoyed in several South American countries. It is served in a gourd and sipped through a silver *bombilla*, resembling a drinking straw with a bulbous end pierced by small holes that strain the leaves. It is commonly spelled maté in the U.S. perhaps because without the accent on the 'e' it becomes mate. In Spanish, the accent on the 'e' changes the pronunciation and the meaning.

bars to do so. He struggled to get it out again, remembering how his ears hurt with trying.

* * *

My first meeting with Sara Méndez was at a busy downtown café in Montevideo.

Sara is a petite woman, with a pretty face surrounded by glossy brown hair. She gestures little—unlike most Uruguayans—and, like Blanca, beneath her gentle and reserved manner I sensed a steely core of strength. We soon discovered that during my research I had, unknowingly, been in touch via email with her husband Raúl, a human rights activist. Before we parted, she invited me to her house, and it was there, that she would tell me the extraordinary story of her search for her son Simón.

* * *

Colonel Ego Correa Luna (retired) was one of a group of young friends who I met on the beaches in summer and danced with at the Saturday night *fiestas*. An accomplished guitarist and composer, he often brought his guitar to our gatherings.

He is unequivocal in his defense of the military's actions against the guerillas.

In a perfect example of *"somos pocos y nos conocemos,"* he tells me of an occasion when he was part of a military force sent to control a student demonstration.

One of the leaders of the demonstration happened to be Jorge, one of the friends he saw at our weekly dances. Coronel Correa Luna—who held no high rank at the time—appealed to their old friendship and asked Jorge to disperse the demonstrators before the military had to take action. Jorge did not disguise his contempt of his old friend and refused to act.

The pain in the Colonel's voice is touching as he tells me this, as if that youthful bond forged on beaches and at dances would hold even when he and Jorge found themselves on opposite sides of a conflict that would soon turn deadly.

Before I leave his home, he gives me two massive books containing a history of military interventions, armed conflicts with guerillas, and photographs. They are no longer in print, so it isn't something he can easily replace, but he wants me to have them, to study them and to understand his point of view. I promise that I will do so. Perhaps because I too cherish the innocence we were privileged to enjoy when we were both very young, I do not judge him.

CHAPTER I

*Guard well that which you cherish but remember that a generous
heart is what makes what you cherish worth guarding.*

**WILLIAM F. SCHULZ, EXECUTIVE DIRECTOR (1994-2006),
AMNESTY INTERNATIONAL USA**

T he silence in the old church was being broken this afternoon
by three young women busily tying white ribbons on the
benches closest to the aisle, an activity they had chosen because it
distanced them from their mothers, who were arranging flowers
by the altar. The girls' voices and laughter rose every so often, sub-
siding when the grownups hushed them.

Emilia, Carla, and Sara did their best to speak quietly but it
became difficult after Emilia discovered a black velvet box in one
of the side altars. She opened it and gasped. It was lined in white
satin and contained seven plain gold bands.

"Emilia, Sara," she whispered, gesturing wildly to her friends
to join her. "Come here!"

They crowded round the box.

"Those look like wedding rings," Emilia said.

"They are," Carla explained. "When my sister Mercedes takes
her vows tomorrow as a bride of Christ, she'll receive one of these."

"Nuns get wedding rings?" Emilia asked, slipping one of the
bands onto her finger.

"They marry Jesus. Put that back Emi!"

"How can anyone marry God?" Emilia had recently become skeptical about religion and never missed an opportunity to question its tenets.

A male voice from the depths of a nearby pew startled the girls. "She can't. It's all part of their superstition."

Sara had been silent until now but as a young man sat up and faced them, his reddish-brown hair tousled as if he had been roused from sleep, she stopped her work. "What are you doing here, Mauricio?"

"Crying," he said.

"You're not."

"Inside I am. My heart is broken."

"You didn't love Carla's sister that much."

"Didn't I?"

"You took up with someone else the day Mercedes entered the novitiate."

"Who told you that?"

The sound of resolute footsteps resounded behind Sara, and Mauricio stood up hastily.

"Mauricio *el rojo*, in a church!" Carla's mother said as she marched toward him. "Is the world coming to an end?"

"Mine is," Mauricio answered.

"He is grieving," Sara said.

"For himself?"

Sara's eyes filled with tears. She'd had a soft spot for him from the moment she met him at a dance party. It wasn't his looks, although he was nice looking enough with his reddish hair and big brown eyes. It was his vulnerability, something lost and searching. Mercedes had laughed when Sara mentioned this boyish quality and said that Sara would soon revise her opinion if she saw Mauricio leading a meeting. His nickname, *el rojo,* the Red, was not just because of his hair. Mauricio was an ardent socialist, Mercedes said, and he gave speeches, organized marches, and was part of a group that planned to take over the country.

Sara's tears only made Carla's mother, Violeta, angrier at Mauricio. "What is it about you that makes all the girls cry? Go home!"

Emilia's mother, Ester, also left the altar to join in ousting Mauricio from the church. "Can't you see that this is a holy day for this family?" Ester said. "Have some manners!"

"You left home, and broke your mother's heart," Violeta said, "living in your workshop like a boy without a family!"

"Sara knows why I left home. She's going to join my group."

Nothing he could have said would have incensed Carla's mother more. She took another step toward Mauricio and shook her finger at him. "If you corrupt these girls with your communist ideas!—"

"I'm not a communist."

Mauricio looked at Sara, held up his hands in mute apology, and walked away. His elbow stuck out through a hole in his sweater, making Sara want to run after him and sew the sweater up tight with both of them inside it.

* * *

There was nothing more romantic, Carla told her friend Mary next day, than the way Mauricio had managed to steal into the church and into one of the side altars to watch her sister Mercedes take her vows.

"He even put on a suit and tamed his hair with gel," Emilia added.

The girls were walking along the Rambla, the promenade running along the shores of Montevideo, Uruguay's capital city. Their friend Mary had joined them, wanting to hear all about the ceremony and Mauricio's appearance at the church. Summer was in the air, and they were wearing short sleeves and had loosened their hair, enjoying the warm breeze blowing off the river after the hours they had spent in their stuffy high school classrooms. They were headed toward a bus stop where each would catch a bus to separate destinations. Sara had not revealed where she was going, but Carla and Emilia were meeting their boyfriends for a coffee. Mary was going to the orphanage near her house where she volunteered twice a week.

"The children are always so glad to see us," Mary said. "Whenever we have money, we take them to the carousel at the Parque Rodó. They love all the rides, especially the roller coaster. And they cry when we leave. I wish I could adopt them all!"

"One time," Emilia said, "my mother and I were walking by the orphanage and a little girl who was playing outside came up to her and put her arms around her. 'Take me with you!' she said, 'take me with you!' It nearly broke my heart. 'Why can't we take her?' I asked my mother. She said it was complicated, you can't just pick up a child like you can a dog or a cat. You have to educate a child, give her a good home."

"Here comes my bus! Where are you going, Sara?" Carla asked.

Sara said she was going home, but she wasn't. She was going to Mauricio's workshop for her first political meeting. She forgave herself the lie by telling herself that she was indeed going home, but not immediately.

Although it was a small gathering of half a dozen people, they had to sit on the concrete floor, since Mauricio owned only two chairs, which at the moment served as tables for plates of pizza and two large bottles of Coca-Cola.

Big posters of Fidel Castro and Che Guevara covered most of the artwork on the walls. Mauricio was studying ceramics, and around the posters and arranged on all sides of them hung a wide variety of pieces, from surrealist shapes, to birds in flight. Sara tried to ignore the icy cold that seeped up from the floor and focus on the conversation going at high intensity around her. US bombers had attacked Hanoi; race riots had been reported in Cleveland, Newark and Detroit; Israel and the Arab nations were at war. But it was the death of Che Guevara in Bolivia a few weeks before, on October 9, 1967, that predominated. Mauricio's older brother, Gerardo, took out a notebook and quoted the words Che had spoken at the Latin American Student Congress in Havana that year. "The future would seem luminous and near if we could see two, three, many Vietnams flowering across the surface of the globe, with their quota of death and their great tragedies, with their daily heroism, and repeated blows against imperialism."

"The old argument about whether or not to take up arms to further our political aims must be put to rest once and for all," Mauricio declared. "It is imperative to create an army of the people to oppose the armies representing imperialism!"

How to explain this need to "the masses" was the burning question of the moment. Unlike Cuba, Uruguay had a long democratic tradition, and most people had no idea what Mauricio and Gerardo were talking about when they proposed liberating them. Mobilizing a comfortable, staunchly middle-class population into a Cuban-style revolution would be a major enterprise.

Known as the Switzerland of Latin America, Uruguay had traditionally been ruled by representatives of two leading political parties: the National Party, commonly referred to as the *Blancos* (the Whites), and the *Colorados* (the Reds—the name bears no relation to communism). The *Blancos* were considered the more conservative of the two parties, with strong support in rural areas. The *Colorados* were urban-based and enjoyed the support of city dwellers and labor unions. Smaller political parties of all stripes, including the Communist Party, also fielded candidates and appeared on the ballot sheets.

The country's social programs provided a free education for all citizens from preschool through university; health care and pensions were guaranteed; all beaches were public and available year-round for walks in the winter and bathing in summer, and cultural activities were widespread and easily accessed. Fond of the good life, Uruguayans sat down to *asados*, consuming generous portions of some of the best beef in the world, and to Sunday lunches of pasta provided by the country's Italian immigrants. Ravioli, spaghetti, gnocci, all seasoned with a variety of red and white sauces, and accompanied by crusty breads, and cheeses from Colonia Suiza—a prosperous community of Swiss immigrants who made and sold dairy products from their small town near the capital—were also enjoyed.

Mauricio's group debated how they would explain that it was ultimately to everyone's advantage for the state to retain control of a country's natural resources, banks, and vital services, such as electricity and water. Clearly, the capitalist model of privatization enriched only the owners and large shareholders, not the people; and further, the debts the country was incurring in order to join the capitalist, developed world—over-developed, Mauricio maintained—would bring ruin upon them all. Contractors, often foreign, had got rich off building dams and selling agricultural equipment that ultimately benefited only a few, while the countries themselves only incurred more and more crippling debt. There was no question among those gathered that once they were in charge, such debts would not be honored.

Sara listened intently to these arguments and found herself agreeing with most of them. Even the Catholic Church to which she had belonged since she was in her mother's womb had turned its attention recently to the poor and dispossessed. Pope John

XXIII had opened up the church and reached out to the laity. Devout men like Sara's father had been encouraged to take a more active part in church matters, assisting priests during religious ceremonies and teaching the gospel. In her early teens, Sara had joined discussion groups, where the role of the Christian in "modifying reality" was examined. No longer were Catholics told to accept God's will unquestioningly. Where economic or civil injustice was concerned they were encouraged to participate actively in bringing about changes that would benefit their communities as a whole. Many priests were in the forefront of revolutionary movements and had an organization of their own—the Movement of Priests for the Third World.

The room grew quiet as Mauricio cautioned them about the dangers of the struggle they were undertaking. Word had leaked out that political prisoners were being mercilessly interrogated in Brazil and Argentina, and that the use of torture was now common. The techniques used to ferret out and question members of leftist organizations were defended by the police and the military by pointing to the words of Brazilian guerrilla Carlos Marighella: "The main task of the urban guerrilla is to distract, wear down, and demoralize the Armed Forces, plus attack, rob from, and destroy foreign enterprises, particularly North American ones." Those engaged in urban guerrilla activities, the authorities said, were terrorists, and should be treated accordingly. "But," Mauricio said, "remember what Marighella said—'No one should be put off by the term terrorist.' On the contrary, it should be a proud title, since today being a terrorist is ennobling for any man, because it signifies a revolutionary attitude. We are engaging in a class war, as urban guerrillas."

"We will fulfill two essential functions," Mauricio's brother Gerardo said. "The liquidation of members of the Armed Forces and police, and the expropriation of money necessary to carry out our guerrilla functions. We will learn to use weapons, to drive a variety of vehicles, to understand technology, and to produce false documentation. As urban guerrillas, we will play an active part in demonstrations and marches, and we must be prepared to meet out justice."

"By this," Mauricio added, "we mean that the urban guerrilla must be prepared to kill."

An even deeper silence fell on the room.

"We are not talking about random violence," Mauricio added. "The Irish Republican Army is not our model."

"Bringing someone to justice," Gerardo said, "is a secret action in which the least number possible of urban guerrillas participates. No one will be obliged to perform an execution, but you need to understand that executions may be necessary."

"Another of our tools," Mauricio continued, "will be kidnapping, done mainly for ransom and exchanging the victim for the freedom of our jailed companions. And have no illusions about this. If you join us, many, perhaps all of you, will be jailed."

Mauricio was a realistic young man, who held few illusions about the dangers surrounding the revolution, but even he had no concept of the forces that would be unleashed against them, and in his wildest dreams could not have imagined the methods that would be employed to wipe them off the face of the earth.

* * *

A few months after Mercedes took her vows, Sara was invited to Carla's house to celebrate Mercedes' first visit home. It would have been more romantic for Carla to report that her sister looked lovesick and wan, but the opposite was true. Mercedes was evidently very happy and in the best of health, and tucked into two helpings of homemade raviolis and several buttered rolls. It was, the girls agreed, Carla's other sister, Josefina, who looked poorly. She had a boil on her neck, covered with a band aid. She had also evidently been to the hairdresser. Her abundant brown hair was piled into a mountain of intricate curls, sprayed until they shone like a plastic dome on her head. Alejandro, the youngest in the family, was taking full advantage of the fact that his strict elder brother Antonio was not with them, to stand behind Josefina and attempt to pierce the dome with a piece of uncooked spaghetti.

His mother Violeta slapped his hand. "Behave yourself!"

Carla's father proposed a toast, "To Sister María de las Mercedes on her six-month anniversary as a bride of Christ!"

Everyone joined in, and when they put their glasses down, Violeta announced that there would be another wedding soon. "Mark my words!"

"What?" Alejandro said. "Carla has managed to catch somebody?"

Carla swatted him with her napkin. "Very funny!"

"I was talking about Josefina," Violeta said.

Carla laughed. "Her tin soldier has proposed?"

"*Mamá*!" Josefina said. "I warn you, if they start—"

"No quarrelling at the table!" Carla's father shouted, brandishing a knife.

Josefina pointed at Alejandro. "It's him and Carla! We'd all get along fine if they'd shut up! Why do they have to make fun of everyone?"

"Not everyone, Josefina," Alejandro said. "But Sergio!" He sat up very straight and brushed the breadcrumbs off his shirt front. "I am Lieutenant Sergio Reyes. An officer and a gentleman. A slave to duty and—"

"*Mamá*!" Josefina shrieked.

Violeta was doing her best not to laugh. "*Corazón*, I love Sergio, he's been our neighbor all our lives, but even you must admit that he has become a little rigid in his ways."

"Not everyone is a leftist like Alejandro!"

"Me?" Alejandro looked astonished.

"You and Carla, and that good for nothing Mauricio. When they start planting bombs, we'll be glad that men like Sergio are here to defend us!"

Carla's father was nonplussed. "Carla and Mauricio want to plant bombs?"

Sara looked at Mercedes, but she was mopping up the last of her tomato sauce with every appearance of enjoyment and as if nothing at all had been said against her former boyfriend. Feeling that someone had to defend him, Sara said, "He just wants us to follow Fidel Castro and free ourselves, *don* Ramón."

"From what?"

As Violeta and Josefina got up to clear the table, Sara launched into an explanation of how the United States and the Soviet Union's competition for control of the so-called third world countries had to be countered by following Cuba's example. Much as *don* Ramón would have enjoyed engaging in a political debate, it was difficult to be heard over the sounds of crockery and silverware and Alejandro's ongoing protests.

"I'm not a communist," he shouted at Josefina as she disappeared into the kitchen, "but if ever Sergio and that friend of his— what's his name? Gavazzo? If ever those two take over the country, I'm joining the comrades!"

"What's wrong with Sergio's friend?" Mercedes asked, having mopped up the last of the ravioli while she waited for dessert.

"He's sinister!"

"I think you've been watching too many Hollywood movies, Alejandro," Sara laughed.

"Have you seen the guy? He wears dark glasses in the rain! He has a vicious Doberman! And his clothes—"

"Definitely too many movies!" Carla said. "Keep him at home

studying, *papá*!"

"It's true! The guy's a Nazi! Isn't he, Sara?"

"I've never met him," Sara said.

"He's a killer!"

Josefina ran out of the kitchen and slapped the back of her brother's head. "How can you let him talk like that, *papá*?"

Alejandro howled, clutching his head, while *don* Ramón banged on the table, spilling salt, pepper and wine on the table-cloth. "Enough! All of you! Look!" he said, gesturing toward Violeta, who was bringing in the dessert, "your mother made flan! Let's eat it in peace!"

The doorbell rang just then, creating a welcome diversion. Violeta, wiping her hands on her apron, hurried to answer. From the dining room, they saw Sergio and his friend Nino Gavazzo standing in the doorway. Josefina left the table and ran to the door to greet her fiancée. Sergio was neatly dressed as always, in tailored gray wool pants and a handsome light blue sweater. Gavazzo was wearing a black leather jacket, boots, and dark glasses. A large Doberman stood at his side.

"Sergio!" Violeta said. "What a nice surprise!"

"Mrs. Velasco, I'd like you to meet my friend, Nino Gavazzo."

"A pleasure," Violeta said, wanting to ask them in but not knowing how to exclude the dog from the invitation.

"May I leave my dog tied up out here?" Nino asked.

Violeta agreed with relief and ushered the two young men into the house. Alejandro made a quick exit, waiting only to be intro-duced, saying he was meeting friends at the movies.

Room was made at the table, and in spite of *don* Ramón and Violeta's efforts to steer the conversation onto safe topics like fam-ily and friends, Nino was soon telling them about a citizens' peti-tion that had recently been brought before Uruguay's Chamber of Deputies. It required that two of their members be relieved of their duties after attending a conference in Havana at which it was determined that a Marxist-Leninist revolution should be imposed by force of arms on the people of Latin America.

Don Ramón expressed his belief that guerrilla warfare was impossible in a small country like Uruguay where there were no mountains or jungles in which anyone could muster forces or remain concealed.

"We're already in a guerrilla war, Mr. Velasco," Nino said. "An urban guerrilla war led by these terrorists calling themselves Tupamaros."

"A few shootouts don't constitute a war, Nino," *don* Ramón said.

"No, sir, but I very much doubt that they'll stop there. These foreign ideas are insidious. Many young people think that when they associate with the Tupamaros they're doing something noble, fighting for the oppressed, that kind of thing."

"It isn't only the Tupamaros who are influenced by foreign ideas," Sara said.

"Paraguay is sending officers to the School of the Americas for brainwashing by the Yankees!" Carla added.

Nino took off his dark glasses. The coldness of his stare cut off anything else the girls might have wanted to say. "How interesting that you should mention that. Sergio and I have just learned that we are to be given the opportunity of being 'brainwashed,' as you put it."

Sergio, who until then had been much more interested in Josefina than in the conversation, stood up. "Yes!" he laughed. "Yes, we are! And we should be going, we have some shopping to do for my mother."

"Remember, young ladies," Nino said addressing himself to Carla and Sara, "that those who take up arms against the state only provide the main spectacle. It's society that creates guerrilla movements, and society that is ultimately responsible for them."

"Using that criteria," *don* Ramón said, moving to stand by his daughter, "one can declare war on entire populations. A dangerous philosophy, don't you think?"

Nino stood up to leave. "A realistic one, if you'll forgive me, sir. The enemies of our way of life can be found in the very heart of our communities. My job, as a defender of the nation, is to find them and root them out."

* * *

"So Sergio and his friend are going to Panama?" Mauricio asked Sara.

They were in Mauricio's workshop, a place Sara was growing to love almost as much as she loved him. Here she could participate in satisfying conversations with people of like mind, away from the supervision of teachers and parents. Mauricio was only a few years older than she and unmarried, but already he had this bohemian hideout all his own which allowed him to meet whoever he pleased at any time of the day or night.

An empty bottle of Coca-Cola was lying on the floor along with the remains of some sandwiches, and the people already there were putting the finishing touches to signs that read, "We shall overcome!" "No more economic imperialism!" "Peace and socialism!" She saw that a fire was roaring in the fireplace, and that the concrete floor was covered in hides. There had been a time in Uruguay's history when hides were cheap, but that was no longer the case. They were in style now, and their value had gone up accordingly. Mauricio had sold a set of masks and bought the hides to celebrate. He had also acquired an old black leather sofa and turned it into something, if not exactly beautiful, at least interesting. He had bought the largest blue and white poncho he could find and draped it over the sofa's most deteriorated parts, giving it a rakish air. He couldn't afford electricity, so the room was lit with the soft glow of kerosene lanterns. The posters that had covered the walls the first time Sara attended a meeting were gone, leaving Mauricio's artwork in view. Masks, vases, bowls, picture frames and mirrors now reflected the firelight.

Sara told Mauricio what she had heard about Sergio and Nino going to the School of the Americas. "What exactly do they do there?" she asked him.

"According to the United States," Mauricio said, "the military are being trained to fight terrorism—and communism—which to them is the same. They fear—and they're right—that we may find Fidel more compelling than Rockefeller, and the loans the Americans want us to take out so we can sell people on the illusion that they want to live like the Americans do. If they can persuade us to become a consumer society then we'll need money to do it, and who has money? The US! And they'll lend it to us," he laughed, "so we can mortgage our future and be in their debt forever."

The signs were finished, and the group began their goodbyes. Sara moved to pick up her coat. "I'll see you at the march tomorrow."

"I'll walk you home."

"My parents would kill me if they knew where I've been. I'll take the bus. They think I'm studying with a friend."

"You are," Mauricio smiled, and gave her a casual goodbye kiss on the cheek.

Sara kissed him back. Mauricio pulled away, surprised by the warmth of her response. She grabbed her coat and ran out of the workshop, slamming the door. She did not stop running until she reached the bus stop. There had been nothing to his kiss, it was simply a goodbye kiss. Why had she tried to turn it into something? She had ruined everything. Perhaps now he thought that her interest in the movement was false, that he was all that had drawn her to the meetings. She would never be able to come back to that room that had become like a second home. Never sit with him discussing the future and their plans for the revolution and the better world that would follow. Apart from losing him as a friend, she had probably forfeited his trust as well.

Before facing him again, she would prove that while she might have been guided and taught by him, the conclusions she had reached and her commitment to the cause were her own.

Too embarrassed to return to the meetings, she focused all her attention on her university studies, and joined a different group, the *Federación Anarquista Uruguaya* (the Uruguayan Anarchist Federation), or FAU.

Her parents had often worried about what they called Sara's doggedness. It didn't seem possible that so much willpower could exist within such a small frame. From the moment she was born, Sara attacked life with both hands. Learning to walk, she had pulled herself up with determination fall after fall; sports she had tackled with an equally intense concentration; and she was never satisfied with any grade below *sobresaliente* (outstanding) in her studies.

Now, Sara threw herself wholeheartedly into the FAU's varied operations, which included the stealing of wigs and hairpieces for use as disguises, and the theft of toys for distribution to poor children. The group moved on to placing tar bombs at political party headquarters. They carried out several bank holdups designed to fund their various activities, among which was identifying people with large accounts. Several FAU members would hold the victim captive at his home or workplace while others went off to cash the check he had been forced to write. Among their more notorious escapades was the theft of a flag from the historical museum at the Cerro fortress. This was not just any flag. This was the flag carried in 1825 from Argentina by thirty-three exiled *orientales* (Uruguayans) who mounted an expedition to free their homeland from a Portuguese invasion, a feat that led to Uruguay's independence. The FAU identified strongly with this small, brave band of men who had stood up to one of the superpowers of the colonial age, and had adopted the flag as its own. Historians, politicians, and patriots of all stripes were outraged by what they saw as a theft of their cultural heritage and the defamation of a national relic. It was not long before the FAU was declared illegal under a constitutional provision outlawing any group that advocated violence. The FAU's modest activities were soon overshadowed by the Tupamaros, the group to which Mauricio and his brother Gerardo belonged. They proceeded to relieve the wealthy Maihlos tobacco family of five hundred thousand dollars and fifty thousand English pounds in gold.

The Tupamaros were soon building "People's Prisons" where they planned to hold captives for ransom. They also targeted two luxurious casinos: the Hotel Carrasco in Montevideo, from which they made off with twenty-five thousand dollars; and the Casino San Rafael in the upscale resort of Punta del Este, where they netted two hundred and twenty thousand dollars. The money was used to buy weapons and establish the hideouts needed as more and more of their members were forced to enter what they referred to as "clandestinity"—a way of life that consisted of living in hideouts and ceasing all contact with family and friends.

No one quite knew how to deal with the Tupamaros, who on June 21, 1969, set the offices of General Motors on fire, and damaged a dozen other United States-owned companies. Under pressure from the United States, the government decided that the police alone could no longer deal with the unrest. Two weeks after the attack, the Uruguayan government brought in the military to assist them. Rather than make the military adhere to the same civil laws that governed the police, the reverse was done, with the police operating in accordance with military codes of conduct. Reflecting the military's conviction that the media had been making heroes of the Tupamaros, and treating their activities as a modern version of Robin Hood and his merry men—and women in this case—the media were immediately informed that henceforth no reference could be made to "subversive actions," and no printed material alluding to Tupamaro or any other guerrilla activity could be introduced into the country.

In neighboring Argentina, a general strike had been called to protest the military government established there in 1966, and urban guerrillas had begun to operate in Buenos Aires. Groups of them also became active in the provinces, stealing uniforms and arms, and holding up banks to finance their operations. One of the principal guerrilla groups that would be formed in Argentina was the ERP: the *Ejército Revolucionario del Pueblo* (The People's Revolutionary Army). Like the Tupamaros in Uruguay, their main means of financial support became kidnappings for ransom.

CHAPTER II

Fighting a war on terrorism . . . leads us to the delusion that the antagonism we experience is not about our policies and practices but about who we are, about our ideals, what we stand for, and our very existence.

WILLIAM F. SCHULZ, EXECUTIVE DIRECTOR (1994-2006), AMNESTY INTERNATIONAL USA

C arla's father had been inclined to support the left until he met his daughter's boyfriend, a good for nothing troublemaker, in *don* Ramón's opinion. Fernando used the words "revolution" and "armed struggle" in what to *don* Ramón seemed a totally irresponsible manner. What could Fernando possibly understand of either? *Don* Ramón had lost relatives in the Spanish Civil War and had little patience with patriots who believed that wars did anything but create more problems for all concerned, except, *don* Ramón said cynically, those who manufactured and sold weapons. They could make millions and ensure that war never touched them or their children. And here was his youngest daughter in love with a revolutionary, and planning to move to Argentina, a military dictatorship. If that wasn't a recipe for personal disaster, *don* Ramón told his wife Violeta, he couldn't imagine what was.

"It's no use objecting," Violeta said, "they're in love!"

"There's no place for love in a revolution!" *don* Ramón snapped.

"How little he remembers about being young," Violeta told Emilia's mother, Ester. "Revolution is an aphrodisiac!"

Ester and Violeta had been friends since childhood. They had attended the same high school, and even though their lives had taken different turns, and sometimes months would go by when they did not see each other, they always picked up where they had left off. Every time they met, they marveled at the fact that Carla and Emilia, born within a year of each other, had also remained friends long beyond the time when they had played together mainly because their mothers met to drink *mate* and stroll along the *Rambla*.

The two women were knitting, a tradition they had established when they realized that left to chance, they would only see each other once or twice a year. Now they had a regular meeting time—the first Friday of every month, and they took it in turns to host the meeting. Tonight they were at Violeta's house. Since they had already made a lifetime supply of scarves and sweaters for all their relatives, they were now knitting for poor children. *Don* Ramón was in the interior for a few days on a business trip, and Violeta had spent the day sprucing up the house. She and her husband had saved for years to buy the land it sat on, and bit by bit, construction materials had gone into building the three bedrooms, kitchen and bathroom, and the entrance room that served as living room and dining room. They had furnished their home one item at a time, until every room was complete. As soon as their neighbors had seen the new furniture and praised her taste, Violeta covered the sofa and chairs in plastic. There was nothing so fine as velvet, they agreed, and the deep red Violeta had chosen was exceptionally elegant. Violeta could still recall how proud she had felt when the set had been delivered.

On this night, Violeta and Ester's thoughts were focused on their daughters, and they commiserated about the heartache of motherhood.

"If only someone had told me how much *more* everything hurts when it happens to our children," Violeta sighed.

"We try to pass on what we've learned but they have to learn it for themselves all over again. It makes it seem so pointless!"

"It's easy when they're little. We are their world and we can make it safe for them, meet their every need. Now . . . "

They knitted in silence for a few moments, listening to a Beethoven concerto on the radio until the news came on, disturbing the momentary peace of the music. There had been a student demonstration downtown. Shop windows had been broken, rocks thrown at the police, several students arrested. Ester and Violeta looked at one another, put down their knitting, and began telephoning their daughters' friends. None of them were home.

They took up their knitting again, prepared to wait. "Remember that huge protest at the university?" Ester asked, dropping a stitch and cursing under her breath. "Back in September of '64, after the government decided to break diplomatic relations with Cuba?"

"The girls were thirteen. I remember because they were both unmanageable."

"We were living near the university back then. We heard the loudspeakers first, then students running by, chased by mounted police. Some of the students picked up stones. The police drew their sabers and hit them. One of the students fell. The policeman tried to run her down, but his horse veered aside and the girl was saved. Emilia and I saw it all! Some of our neighbors opened their lobby doors to hide the students. Emilia ran down and took in some poor kid with scraped knees who burst into tears as soon as he was safe!"

Violeta crossed herself. "Let's hope that there are still people who dare do that for our kids. Why, why, do they have to do this to us?"

"They're so naïve!" Ester said. "Emi thinks that if the Tupamaros come into power they'll fix everything and there'll be no more poverty; that it's just a matter of wanting to make it happen and having the right people in control. I'm such a cynic, Violeta. I'm afraid that once they're in power, they'll be as bad as the people they replace!"

"You're just like my husband. But the young people want to be involved. They're idealistic, such dreamers. Like Fernando!" Violeta told Ester all about her husband's objections to Carla's boyfriend. "I wish Carla was more like Elena!"

Elena was Violeta's brand-new daughter-in-law, married to Carla's elder brother, Antonio. "Elena is such a good girl—studies hard, dresses neatly—have you noticed how our girls don't seem to care how they look these days?"

"I've given up on Emilia. She won't wear any of the clothes I buy for her."

"They look like those American hippies! But not Elena. She wears gloves, and high heels, she has her hair done and her nails are always polished. She looks like a lady, you know? And she refuses to get involved in politics. All Elena has ever wanted is to get married and have children."

"I didn't know they made them like that anymore."

"Me either. I'm glad that Antonio found her."

"Does Carla like her?"

"Can't stand her."

Ester glanced at her watch. It was well past time for the girls to be home. "I could kill Emilia sometimes," Ester said.

"I think the worry will kill us first," Violeta sighed.

"In my day, if I had been out this late, it would have been to meet a boy! My mother worried that I was losing my virtue. I worry that Emilia is getting arrested! Of all times for my husband to choose to die."

"How did he choose to have a heart attack, poor man?" Violeta said reproachfully. "Really, Ester!"

CHAPTER 11

"He never could discipline Emilia."

"My husband is the same. Carla can do no wrong. Except where her boyfriend Fernando is concerned." Violeta suddenly held up her hand, listening. "The dogs!"

The dogs near the bus stop gave the alarm whenever anyone got off the bus, and Violeta could tell if it was Carla coming, because other dogs picked up the cry as she got closer to home.

"Let's surprise them!" Ester said, jumping up and turning off the light. "They deserve a fright after what they've put us through." They parted the curtains slightly, looking out. Their daughters were approaching the low wall that fronted the street.

"Oh, good!" Carla whispered, seeing the dark house. "It looks like my mother has gone to bed."

Emilia reached for the gate.

"Don't! It creaks." Carla gestured for her to climb over the low wall. "Be careful with the roses! My mother will kill us if we step on them."

Once in the little front garden, Carla took out her key and inserted it carefully in the lock, opening the door slowly. As they stepped into the room the lights went on.

"¡Ay, mami!" Carla cried. "Must you lurk in the dark and frighten us to death!" Her eyes fell on Ester. "Oh, señora Ester, you're here too!"

"What excuse have you got this time?" Violeta said.

"I called you, mamá," Emilia said to Ester, "but no one answered. I didn't know you were here."

"And here the phone was busy. I tried!" Carla said.

"Do you know why the phone was busy?" Violeta said. "Because while we were listening to the news, we heard there'd been another demonstration. So we were calling all your friends trying to find you."

"We can't go on like this, girls." Ester said.

"I'm sorry, *mamá*," Emilia said. "But we're well off. We have homes and plenty of food. We must think of those who don't."

"This is Uruguay!" Ester said. "Who starves? No one!"

"Times are hard," Violeta admitted, "but those who want to can still find work."

"I'm not giving this up, *mamá*," Carla said. "I've been searching for it for a long time."

"What is this 'it'?" Violeta said, throwing up her hands.

"We're working to establish a new political order."

"You're communists?" Violeta cried.

"They're too tame for us!" said Emi. "They want to do it through elections."

"And what's wrong with that?"

"They'll fail," Emilia said. "They have to follow all the political party rules to run in the elections."

"By the time they've been through the system," Carla added, "they'll be the same as everybody else."

Ester sat down. "This is dangerous thinking, girls."

"What is life without a little danger?" Emilia laughed.

"Wait till you're a mother then ask yourself that question!" Violeta retorted.

"One of the speakers at today's demonstration said that when one dreams one must give oneself to the bone!" Emilia said.

"He is obviously not a mother," Ester sighed.

* * *

Violeta had been right about the fact that there would soon be a wedding in the family; upon his return from the School of the Americas in Panama, Sergio and Carla's sister Josefina became engaged. They had grown up together, running in and out of one another's houses, playing ball at the beach, and dancing together at parties. When Sergio joined the army as a young recruit, fighting guerrillas had been the furthest thing from his mind, and joining guerrillas had not yet occurred to Carla. When rumors of a guerrilla movement began to circulate in Uruguay, Sergio felt a mixture of anger and fear: anger at anyone who would dare upset his orderly, mapped-out life, and fear of the disruption that would follow, and his reaction to it. Was it possible that he was afraid of fighting, of dying? He had joined the Armed Forces, for heaven's sake. What did that indicate if not a willingness to die for his country? It was what he had been trained to do. But the worst he had ever imagined was that he might be called upon to perform a peace-keeping mission in some far-off place. The idea that he might have to fight his own countrymen was abhorrent to him, particularly if they were his neighbors, former classmates, even members of his family. He wished he were more like Nino, for whom these issues seemed so straightforward. Anyone siding with the Tupamaros was the enemy, all former ties erased. For Nino a line had been drawn. On one side were the righteous, himself included, and on the other the evil-doers, those who questioned everything Nino had been taught to believe. Sometimes, Sergio envied his friend's ability to simplify issues that Sergio found more complex. Did it all come down to a hunger for power, as Nino claimed? Nino even maintained that the communists, who he believed were behind all the unrest, were in control of the Catholic Church.

"That's nonsense!" Sergio said.

"Think about it. Lenin said that the Church should not be confronted, it should be infiltrated, and now here's the Pope taking a militant stance on what he calls social justice."

"You don't think the Pope is a communist?"

"He seems to be encouraging them. Listen to this." Nino pulled a newspaper clipping from his pocket. "Third World bishops have issued a manifesto declaring that 'revolutions that promote human rights are bearers of the values proclaimed by the gospel.'"

"Don't you agree that human rights should be promoted?"

"Listen to their language, Sergio! They've gone so far as to say that the Church does not wish to be linked to financial imperialism. Those are communist words! And that bunch calling themselves the Movement of Priests for the Third World are just using the church as a shield. They join the guerrillas all over Latin America, pretending to fight for 'the people' when all they're after is power for themselves."

"I didn't like what I saw at that last demonstration," Sergio said. "The students were unruly, yes, they were destructive and insolent, but they were, after all, just students."

"Didn't you learn anything in Panama, Sergio? Sure, some of them are students, but their leaders, the ones pulling the strings, are Castro's communists! Who do you think is master minding all the bank holdups, the casino robberies—kids? Their professors, my friend, their priests and Castro's puppets."

"Then what did we accomplish by chasing them down, by beating them, by hauling them off to jail?"

"What else could we do? Stand by and watch while they destroy our country?"

So far no one had been seriously hurt in the encounters between the guerrillas and the police, but the rumbles in military barracks were increasing, and Nino's was one of the loudest voices. He admired the Brazilian military for staging a coup there, and worried that Argentina's Junta wasn't going to hold out, that they would give in to pressure to hold elections. As for Chile, Nino's dark eyes seemed to turn even darker whenever anyone mentioned Communist presidential candidate Salvador Allende.

* * *

1970 was an eventful year for South Americans. Just as Nino had feared, Argentina's military returned to barracks, and elections were held; and in Chile, Salvador Allende was elected President. When the news of Allende's victory was broadcast, demonstrations and celebrations broke out all over South America. If Cuba could oust Batista*, and Chile could elect Allende, anything was possible, and the future surely bright for socialism in the southern continent.

The military had better watch out! Mauricio's brother Gerardo said. No longer would they be allowed to step in and overthrow anyone who didn't please them or the imperialist powers they served.

The celebrations did not last long. Immediately after Allende's election, disturbing rumors began to fly. Mauricio learned that Richard Helms, Director of the CIA, had been in touch with Chilean General Roberto Viaux Marambio about the unsettling turn of events in his country. The general was quite willing to put himself at Helms' service and prevent Allende from taking office, but there was one formidable barrier—General René Schneider, head of the army and staunch defender of his country's constitution. So long as General Schneider was in charge, the army would defend a duly elected president, even if they abhorred his politics. These "constitutional military," as they were called, were assuming a risky stance, Mauricio said, since those in the know in Chile had heard that the US had paid a far-right terrorist group to kill General Schneider.

Until two days before the Chilean Congress was due to confirm Salvador Allende as president elect of Chile, all but the most cynical among the guerrillas doubted this story.

---

* Fulgencio Batista first came to power in Cuba in 1933, following a coup. Elected in 1940, he lost power in the 1944 elections, and from his luxurious retreat in Miami put together a second coup in 1952. Fidel Castro tried ousting Batista in 1953 and failed. Imprisoned for two years for his efforts, he planned a second attempt after he was released, and in 1959 succeeded in overthrowing Batista.

The assassination attempt against General Schneider was not immediately successful. Gunned down near his home, the general managed to hang on to life until Allende was confirmed. On the following day, believing the presidency to be secure, the general died.

Up to this point, moderate leftist voices had maintained that for the United States to interfere with a duly elected government was so contrary to everything it stood for that American citizens would never consent to it. They were proved wrong. Many of them joined the extremists or withdrew in shock from an arena where the supposed defenders of democracy were proving to be its worst enemies. The lid was blown off any restraint the guerrillas had so far shown.

Meanwhile, in Uruguay, a major turning point was reached when the Tupamaros decided to kidnap Daniel Mitrione, an employee of the US State Department responsible for introducing sophisticated torture techniques into the country. Born in August of 1920 in Italy, Mitrione became chief of police of Richmond, Indiana. At age 37, he completed his FBI training, and three years later, joined the Department of State as a police trainer overseas. He was assigned to OPS, the Office of Public Safety. Mitrione began his overseas work in Brazil in the early 1960's, when a new kind of prisoner was being brought into military barracks and to out-of-the-way sites run by "special forces operatives." These prisoners were guerrillas, leaders and members of unions, students, and people belonging to religious organizations advocating social justice.

Brazilians would be the last to claim that their prisons were free from abuse. Beatings and rough treatment were common means of getting information out of thieves and murderers. Prior to 1960, however, sophisticated methods of modern torture, such as electric prods and the use of drugs, were not the norm.

Once he had trained "special forces operatives" in Brazil, Mitrione was assigned to do the same in Uruguay. By the time the Tupamaros kidnapped him, some of them had experienced his methods firsthand. In spite of this, restraint in handling Mitrione was the order of the day. He was not to be abused, and the bullet wound he had sustained during his capture was promptly treated by a doctor.

Meanwhile, civilian and military prisons were filling with people accused of being "subversives," and the Tupamaro leadership believed that things had come to such a pass that only the threat of killing Dan Mitrione would make the government negotiate for the release of prisoners. A deadline was announced, but the government did not budge. No negotiations would take place with the Tupamaros, even if they continued to threaten the life of one of their captives. Backed into a corner, the Tupamaros executed Mitrione.

* * *

Sara's parents heard of Mitrione's murder on television. Sara was not home at the time. She had become a teacher and her job was a long bus ride away. When, cold and exhausted, she walked into the house, her parents were ready to confront her.

"Tell me you had no hand in this," her father said, gesturing to the television, where pictures of the Buick convertible in which Mitrione's body had been found were still being flashed on the screen.

"Please, Sara," her mother said.

"I don't want to lie to you. I'm not one of the decision makers, but—"

"Is Mauricio behind this?"

"I haven't seen Mauricio for a long time."

"Do you approve of murder?" her father asked.

"This was an execution."

"What's the difference?"

A similar confrontation was going on between Ester and Emilia, while at Carla's her parents were phoning all her friends. Carla had not come home for the night, and they had barely slept, listening for her key in the door, and looking out the window every time there was a sound in the street. Fernando also failed to appear at his house, and *don* Ramón was certain that Carla was with him and up to no good.

The more he thought about it the angrier he became, until Violeta began to worry that *don* Ramón would enrage himself into an apoplexy. Every time the phone rang, he jumped to answer it and when there was a thump at the front door, *don* Ramón flung it open and stared furiously into empty space. When he saw the newspaper lying at his feet, he kicked it into Violeta's rose bushes. Fearful that the neighbors would see her husband making a spectacle of himself Violeta ran out to collect the sheets of newspaper and was just returning inside when her eye fell on a photograph of Carla with the caption "Tupamaro Collaborator Arrested." She clutched the newspaper, walked into her house, and shut the door firmly behind her.

When *don* Ramón saw the photograph, he locked himself in the bedroom and refused to come out, leaving Violeta to deal with the phone calls from relatives and friends who had also seen the paper and called to offer their condolences, as if Carla were dead.

When the calls finally stopped, Violeta broke down and wept. "What did we do wrong?"

Don Ramón wept with her. "It's all that good for nothing Mauricio's fault! I told you he was trouble the first time I saw him!" He was so ashamed of what had befallen his family that for the next three days he didn't leave the house.

* * *

Violeta didn't know what surprised her more—her eldest son Antonio's wife Elena announcing that they should all visit her sister-in-law in prison, or d*on* Ramón's declaration that Elena was quite right.

Even though it had been her idea, Elena's teeth chattered all the way to the visiting room. It had not crossed her mind, she told Violeta, that she would ever enter the women's prison, let alone to visit a relative.

Much as she adored her daughter, Violeta was embarrassed by the visit. Carla barely glanced at the expensive toiletries Elena had brought her, and her brash and insolent attitude grated on Violeta. Having said that the visit was a good idea, once inside the prison *don* Ramón was bereft of speech. The longer he sat, entrenched in his shame and disappointment, the harder Carla became, boasting of how the jailers feared her and her companions, and of how easy it was to manipulate them by threatening to kidnap relatives on the outside.

"We'd never do it, of course, but they don't know that," she said contemptuously.

"At least," *don* Ramón retorted, "they are earning an honest living. I wish we could say the same for you!"

"I am fighting for the future of the revolution. For the good of the country!"

"You are indulging in a crazy fantasy that is destroying your family!"

"Families have to be sacrificed for the good of society!"

"There is no society without families. And I will not be sacrificed to your selfish idiocy, do you understand me? I hope they keep you in here for a good long time, until you come to your senses!"

By this time Violeta was in tears, so Elena took *don* Ramón away, allowing Carla and her mother a few moments alone together.

Later, when the Uruguayan authorities offered them the option to emigrate, Carla and Fernando chose Chile.

"They'll be stirring up trouble there, no doubt!" *don* Ramón said.

He was right. It soon became apparent that Carla and Fernando were involved in some clandestine activity in their host country, because news of them came only through a cousin who lived in Valparaiso and occasionally received calls from Carla. Calls no one could return, since Carla would not reveal where she was. The last time the cousin had called, it had been to say that Carla and Fernando were safe—and married. *Don* Ramón threw his hands up in despair, and once more refused to go out for three days.

He and Violeta, however, did derive some comfort from Josefina and Sergio's wedding, although they spent many hours asking themselves how it was possible to contain two such diametrically opposed couples within one family.

* * *

In the two years that followed, 1970-72, the Tupamaros continued their guerrilla activities, kidnapping several public figures, including British Ambassador Geoffrey Jackson.

Uruguay was not alone in its time of turmoil.

In Bolivia, General Hugo Banzer Suárez took power in 1971, ushering in the country's fifteenth change of government in seven years, and killing hundreds of peasants in the process. After one of the massacres, the general assured his "brother peasants" that they not only had his permission, but he would assume responsibility for murdering the first "agitator" who arrived in the countryside.

Aided by Nazi war criminal Klaus Barbie, the *Junta* proceeded to make cocaine Bolivia's chief export. Deposed President Torres went to Chile, where he survived an assassination attempt and moved on to Buenos Aires.

In the United States, four students were killed by the National

Guard at Kent State University in Ohio during a Vietnam War protest, and Governor George Wallace of Alabama was shot. England's policies in Northern Ireland continued to result in terrorism in both countries. India and Pakistan were at war, and Arab terrorists targeted the Olympic Games in Munich, resulting in the deaths of two Israeli athletes and nine hostages.

In light of the violence erupting all over the globe, the Vatican declared world justice to be the gravest and most urgent of the day's problems, a situation calling for "a new man, one with the strength necessary to undertake the task of renovation." A task, the Vatican said, that would require changes in lifestyle and in ways of resolving conflict. "A man, in other words, prepared to widen his horizon and embrace humanity in its entirety."

* * *

Gathered as usual on Sundays for a family lunch, Sergio, Josefina, and *don* Ramón lamented that the leadership the Vatican called for was nowhere evident. The women chimed in, declaring that world social unrest and violence would keep escalating and the number of dead mounting, until more women were in positions of power.

Sergio, replete with ravioli, was sitting by the fire reading the paper while the others played cards and drank coffee. "This will go over well," he said dryly, reading from the paper. "Listen to this! The Tupamaros have announced their plan of government. 'Agrarian reform will be instituted by expropriating ranches and large tracts of land.' I can just see our first families standing for that! 'Factories and national industries such as meat and wool will be nationalized.' There go all our sources of income! 'Foreign commerce, imports and exports will be administered by the state.'"

Antonio burst out laughing. "It takes a year to get them to

process one piece of paper! Are they planning to fire everyone and start over? Because if they use the current public employees nothing will ever leave or enter Uruguay until it's obsolete."

"'Savings and loans,'" Sergio continued, "'will be centralized and the economy planned in such a way that production will be financed and speculation eliminated. As for foreign capital, large industries, businesses, and banks totally or partially owned by foreign capital will be appropriated without compensation. The standard of living of all workers will be raised, and education promoted with an emphasis on technology. Private hospitals and drug manufacturing laboratories will be expropriated, and the elderly and the handicapped—anyone who cannot work—will have all their needs met.'"

"We'll be a country of cripples!" *don* Ramón said. "All living off a government that won't buy or sell anything! It'll be our very own miracle."

The Frente Amplio, the party the Tupamaros supported, had made a good showing in the 1971 elections and won 18 percent of the vote. Violence in Uruguay had nevertheless continued to escalate. Money, radio equipment, and arms were stolen; the Golf Club set on fire, and the Chief of Security for the prison of Punta Carretas—from which one hundred and six Tupamaros escaped through an underground tunnel—was shot while waiting for a bus.

The response of Uruguay's new President, Juan María Bordaberry, was to declare a state of internal warfare, handing the fight against "subversives" entirely over to the military to manage. Personal rights and liberties were suspended, including the rights to meet, to belong to unions, and to criticize the way the joint military and police forces were conducting the anti-subversive fight.

The pros and cons of this were lengthily debated, and then,

as occurred at every family reunion, the conversation turned to Carla's situation. Someone should go to Chile to make sure that she was all right, her sister Josefina said. "We weren't even able to say goodbye to her properly and now there she is living in exile in Chile for two years, and all we know about her are those messages she sends through a cousin we've never even met!"

"I would jump on the first plane," *don* Ramón said, "if I could be assured of not seeing Fernando, who I will murder with my bare hands if he ever shows himself."

Violeta said nothing, but Antonio knew that his mother was desperately worried about Carla. Two years was an eternity to her. Violeta's hair had turned gray and she had developed the nervous habit of glancing at the telephone every few minutes. Until the moment his sister Carla was arrested, not a day had gone by when Carla and Violeta had not seen each other or at least spoken on the phone.

Antonio and Elena had discussed going to Chile and Antonio knew that while Elena resented having to spend their money on her irresponsible sister-in-law, she understood that as Carla's elder brother, Antonio felt obligated to volunteer. Perhaps, he told Elena, they could turn it into a second honeymoon.

Family obligations were something Elena perfectly understood. Besides, she had grown very close to Violeta since marrying Antonio and would do anything for her mother-in-law. An only child, Elena had lost her own mother in a car accident when she was nine. Marrying into a large, close-knit family had been a dream come true. They had all, with the exception of Carla, taken her in, accepting and pampering her as they did one another. When she had her appendix removed and spent two nights in the hospital, Antonio's family closed around her like a warm blanket, in attendance day and night at the hospital, doing everything for her once she went home. They did not deserve the worry they were experiencing over Carla, and if she could do anything to relieve it, she would.

When Antonio told his mother of their decision, Violeta threw her arms around them both, sobbing with relief.

* * *

Antonio and Elena were in Chile for three weeks, during which time Carla did not call Antonio once. He felt he should do everything he could to find his sister, but since his only option was to wait for a call, his frustration escalated as the days went by. He dreaded facing his family if he failed to contact his sister, and soon Elena despaired of being able to salvage anything resembling a second honeymoon. But three days before they were due to leave, Antonio said that the waiting was at an end. For the little time left to them in Santiago, they would pretend that Carla did not exist. Paying for a hotel and meals had taken most of their savings, and expensive outings were out of the question, so they walked the city streets, strolled through the plazas, visited museums, went dancing, made love, and recaptured some of the carefree life they had enjoyed before Carla's arrest.

No sooner had they returned to Montevideo than they received a message saying that Carla had turned up and was very sorry to have missed them. Elena could cheerfully have strangled her sister-in-law by then. Instead, she offered to turn right around and return to Chile with Violeta. Antonio could take no more time off from his job or his university studies. There was no money left for plane tickets, so Elena and Violeta traveled by train through Mendoza in Argentina and overland to Santiago.

The journey provided an opportunity for the two women to grow closer. They spoke of their childhoods—Violeta too had lost her mother at a young age—and how both had dreamed of being wives and mothers. Elena revealed a secret despair. She and

Antonio had been married for two years now with no signs of a pregnancy. Violeta told her about all the women she knew who had waited years for a child and then suddenly, miraculously, become pregnant. The same would happen to Elena, she was certain of it.

When the train pulled into the station in Santiago, Carla was there, waiting with a grin. She was civil to Elena and even thanked her for accompanying Violeta, who spent most of the first hour crying. Until she saw Carla at the station, Violeta had feared that her daughter was dead, and that the family had been concealing the truth from her. Violeta's relief at seeing and touching Carla, at hearing her voice after more than two years, almost made up for the fact that Carla made it clear that Violeta and Elena could not visit her or see with whom she was living. She would answer no questions, and appeared unaccompanied at their hotel at all hours of the day and night. No matter the time, Elena would dress, and leave Violeta and Carla alone. Violeta protested, but Elena always found a reason for going out. Carla said nothing, but one night, as Elena was leaving, she caught her eye and Carla nodded. It was the closest to an understanding that the two young women ever came. Elena sensed a change in Carla, an awareness that had not been there before. Until then, Elena would not have thought her capable of understanding how much her absence hurt her mother. Now she had a feeling that these daily visits were a gift Carla was making to Violeta.

Being in Santiago in early 1972 was both exhilarating and frightening. Carla's surreptitious visits and clandestine existence made Elena realize, in a way she had not been sensitive to while she was in Chile with Antonio, that the country was a powder keg, liable to explode at any moment. According to Carla, the United States was funding a destabilization campaign that threatened to bring down not only Allende's government, but Chile's economy as well. Demonstrations for and against the President were ongoing, and one day Elena and Violeta were caught in the midst of one. They took a wrong turn on their way back to the hotel, and before they knew it, they were being pulled along in a growing tide of people carrying signs and flags. At one point, through an opening in the crowd, Elena saw that they were marching toward a similar group of demonstrators bearing down on them from the opposite direction. Some of them had knives tied to the tops of their flags, there was a lot of verbal abuse, and here and there someone was pushed or chased by an opposing demonstrator. Elena decided that if a fight broke out, she would grab her mother-in-law and duck for cover. As the crowd flowed by an apartment building, Elena pulled Violeta into the lobby, where they waited until the last of the demonstrators had gone by. They were shaken when they got back to the hotel, but the worst was yet to come. Violeta's purse was empty, their money and documents gone. Thankfully, their train tickets were in Elena's purse. It was then that Violeta saw the metal of which her daughter-in-law was made. Elena had just enough in her money belt to pay for the hotel and transportation to the train station. Not a *peso* was left to pay the ten dollar a day visitor's fee. By pleading with the customs agent and showing him the police report of the theft of her purse, Elena persuaded him not only to let them leave the country without documents, but to waive the fee.

Their troubles were far from over. Buenos Aires, where they were due to change trains, was in the grip of a general strike. It was pouring rain when they arrived, and nothing was open for business. Even Elena was hard pressed to devise a way out of their predicament. They had left the train station, which was being shut down, and were standing with their bags on a street corner, soaked and shivering, when a well-dressed man approached them.

"Do you need a ride somewhere?" he asked, sheltering them

with his umbrella. "The taxis, you know, are all on strike."

"No, thank you, *señor*," Elena replied, "but we appreciate your kind inquiry."

"Is someone picking you up?"

"Our money and documents were stolen in Santiago," Violeta said. "We are stranded."

"Heavens, why didn't you say so before." He shepherded them under an awning. "I am in town on business, from Córdoba." He took out a handsome, silver card-holder, extracted a card, wrote something on the back, and handed it to Violeta. "I am staying at this hotel, it's only a block away. Go there and tell the concierge to give you a room where you can at least have a shower and some hot coffee. You shall be my guests until the trains are running again."

Violeta and Elena were dumbfounded and afterwards could not remember whether they had even thanked the kind stranger. Fortunately, they had kept his card, and in the years to come, on the anniversary of the day on which, as Violeta put it, they staggered into the hotel like two drowning rats, she and Elena sent their blessings for his kindness.

CHAPTER III

*In Argentina we were influenced first by the French and then
by the United States. We used their methods separately at first
and then together, until the United States' ideas finally predominated. France and the United States were our main sources
of counter-insurgency training. They organized centers for teaching counter-insurgency techniques (especially in the US) and sent
out instructors, observers, and an enormous amount of literature.*

GENERAL JUAN ALBERTO CAMPS, *THE DEFEAT OF
SUBVERSION: THE RISE AND FALL OF GUERRILLA GROUPS
IN ARGENTINA.*

I n the early morning, light frost glistened on the grass outside
the rural schoolhouse where Sara was doing her student teaching, and soon, from all directions, children on foot and horseback
began to make their way toward the small building. The children's
shoes and satchels ranged from good to poor condition. Some
wore socks and sweaters under their white regulation tunics, and
coats over them, but many did not, so Sara had arrived early to
light the kerosene heater and make the room as warm and welcom-
ing as she could.

On a small table she was heating milk on an electric grill.
Today, thanks to Ester and Violeta's efforts, there was a mound
of hand-knitted sweaters to distribute. The last time, Sara had

simply given them to whomever she thought needed them, and noticed that some of the children had seemed embarrassed at being singled out. So this time, she had talked it over with one of the other teachers, a colleague named Raúl, and he had come up with the idea of a raffle. They had pooled their money and bought pencils, crayons, and a brand new pair of sneakers, and asked Ester and Violeta to knit scarves, gloves, and socks to add to the drawing. Sara had no qualms about engaging in a little judicious rigging of the raffle, so that the warm clothes and shoes went to those children who needed them the most.

At the end of the day, everyone left with something, and Sara was congratulating herself on how smoothly it had gone, when the school principal came into the room to tell her that there was a phone call for her in the office.

Sara had barely said hello when a voice interrupted. "They're at your house. Go straight to the ferry."

Sara had not heard Mauricio's voice for almost three years. The sound of it brought back the stab of pain that had accompanied the last piece of news she had received about him. He was married, someone had told her, to a woman also living in hiding. Sara had no opportunity to pull herself together, or to speak, before the connection was cut off.

Three hours later, in an effort to still her trembling, she pushed her hands into the pockets of her light coat as she waited in line to buy a ticket for the ferry to Buenos Aires. Her colleague Raúl had lent her enough money for the ferry, and insisted on giving her more. She could pay him back later, Raúl said. She still regretted the danger she had put him in by confiding in him, but there had been no one else in the rural school house to whom she could turn, and from the comments he had made to her in the past, she suspected that his sympathies lay with the guerrillas, not the military.

Sara was so engrossed in her thoughts that she did not notice the people in the line behind her stepping away.

"Visiting Buenos Aires, are you?" Sergio, in full army uniform, was at her elbow.

"Do any of your new laws forbid it?" she answered, surprised by how calm she sounded.

"In your case, they do. I came to warn you. You are safer here than you will be in Buenos Aires."

"I should trust our military over a democracy?"

"If you are under any illusions about Argentina's allegiance to democracy, abandon them."

They had almost reached the ticket counter. When Sergio saw her counting out her money, he took out his wallet. "I'm buying you a two-way ticket." Sara began to object. He silenced her, gesturing to the money in her hand. "A one-way ticket and no luggage? Suspicious, don't you think? I won't always be able to protect you, Sara. Use me while you can."

* * *

Sara's first night in Buenos Aires had been a lonely one. She had never been away from home for longer than a few days, and had never slept anywhere except in her own bed or at the home of a relative. Her family and childhood friends had always been near, her surroundings familiar. Now here she was in a city five times the size of Montevideo, at the home of a couple who formed part of a network that received political exiles and housed them until they found the means to support themselves. She would not have thought it possible to miss anything or anyone with the intensity with which she longed for her home and family from the moment she arrived in Buenos Aires.

Her first day was spent buying a change of clothing and looking for work, wondering how she would ever learn her way around the vast city and its sprawling suburbs. On her second day, she took the wrong bus and ended up two hours away from her destination. By the time she got back to the house she was almost in tears, and hurried to her room to compose herself. A few minutes later, she heard a knock at the front door and the sound of voices raised in greeting. When Sara went to see who had come, she found Mauricio—his red hair wet from the rain—and his brother Gerardo taking off their backpacks in the front room. Any awkwardness there might have been between them was dispelled in the cacophony of greetings and welcomes, and the exchange of the latest news, which included the fact that Mauricio and his wife had separated. Sara tried not to feel anything at the news, but she could not stem the hope and desire that rushed through her. When Mauricio invited her to have a coffee with him, she accepted.

"I would have preferred telling you myself—and privately—that I'm separated," Mauricio said, stirring sugar into his coffee.

"It didn't surprise me."

"You never even met her!"

"It was you I was thinking of."

"You don't believe me capable of a lasting relationship?"

"Are you capable of it, Mauricio?"

"With someone like you, yes. You're so calm. So certain. Do you know what they call you?"

"I don't want to know."

"It's a beautiful name. Sara the Wise. And I need wisdom, Sara. Could you love me?"

She should have resisted, made him wait, but she was as incapable of playing games of love as she was of toying with anything she deemed important. When Mauricio asked her if she could love him, there was only one answer.

They found work, she as a nanny, and he in a bottling factory, and they moved in together. Soon the tiny bedroom in their apartment became a temporary haven from homesickness. At least when they made love, they could forget where they were and why.

* * *

A few months after Sara, Mauricio, and Gerardo left Uruguay, the Uruguayan Parliament was dissolved, and a National Security Council created, composed of a few politicians and several military commanders. Uruguayans were urged by President Juan María Bordaberry to remain calm and carry on as usual—an appeal to which citizens responded by calling a national strike. Thousands, including Ester's daughter Emilia and her boyfriend Jorge, took to the streets singing the national anthem, and were met by squadrons armed and equipped with tear gas. The university was placed under military control, with the majority of its teachers, professors and inspectors fired or forced to resign. Hundreds were imprisoned, and many left the country.

On September 11 of that fateful year, 1973, the United States achieved its objective and toppled the government of Chilean President Salvador Allende.

All five nations surrounding Argentina were now under military control.

Sara wrote regularly to Ester, keeping her abreast of events in her own life and in Buenos Aires. President Cámpora, who Sara respected, and who had offered shelter to the many thousands escaping the dictatorships surrounding him, had been forced to resign the leadership of the Peronist Party to its founder, Juan Domingo Perón. He had returned to Argentina from his exile in Spain accompanied by his new wife, Isabel. Peron's arrival provided extremists on the left and right with an opportunity to disgrace themselves. Four hundred people were injured and over a dozen killed in the chaos that ensued. Elected president a few months later, Perón attended his inauguration ceremonies in full military regalia, which as far as Sara was concerned, did not bode well. Neither did the fact that Perón had nominated his wife Isabel as his Vice President. Apart from her status as Perón's wife, Sara wrote to Ester, Isabel had no known qualifications for the job.

Sara did not use the usual post, but sent her unsigned letters hidden inside a book, or under layers of chocolates and in the care of companions she could trust. Perón, she told Ester, soon saw to it that new laws were passed restricting freedom of the press and the right to strike. Perón's valet, José López Rega, nicknamed *el Brujo* (the Sorcerer) had become his secretary, and recently, he had also been named Minister of Social Welfare. His nickname, Sara said, was due to his fascination with the occult, which he passed on to Perón and to his wife Isabel. López Rega was in close contact with European fascists and Nazis, after whom he fashioned the Triple A—the *Alianza Anticomunista Argentina*—The Argentine Anti-Communist Alliance or AAA—which operated secretly. As far as Sara and Mauricio could tell, the AAA consisted of approximately two hundred members, all police and military men on the far right of political thought. The Argentine guerrillas, the *Montoneros*, had told Sara that the Triple A extorted money from people and dealt in drugs. They had no qualms about committing murder and blaming it on the *Montoneros*, who, like the Tupamaros, financed their operation largely with holdups and kidnappings. In 1973, nine foreign executives representing large enterprises in Argentina were held for ransom, a Ford Motor Company representative was killed, and the total number of kidnappings rose to over one hundred and fifty. More than half of the foreign work force left Argentina as a result. Even more disturbing was a report that Perón had authorized the Federal Police and the Argentine intelligence services to cooperate with military intelligence in Chile, Uruguay, Brazil, and Bolivia in arresting exiles from those countries now living in Argentina. Argentina might be a democracy, but it was behaving like a dictatorship. Sara remembered Sergio's parting words to her—"If you are under any illusions about Argentina's allegiance to democracy, abandon them."

I am finding it difficult, Sara wrote, to adjust to my new life. Even though all of you are less than half an hour away by plane, sometimes I feel as if I've moved to another continent, the differences between the two cities are so great. Buenos Aires is huge! Over eight million people live here, compared to which our little Montevideo with its one and a half million, now seems tiny! I miss the close ties between neighbors, the leisurely pace of Montevideo, the ease with which people pause to drink mate and exchange the news of the day.

Ester in turn wrote to tell Sara that Emilia and Jorge were getting married.

I remember all too well how hurt I was by my own parents unenthusiastic response to my choice of a husband, and I don't want to spoil Emi's joy in the same way, but it's impossible for me to celebrate their decision. It isn't that I dislike Jorge. On the contrary, he's intelligent, hardworking, and most importantly, he adores Emi and would do anything for her. But he's just as idealistic as she is, and willing to sacrifice himself to achieve his ideals.

Given the current state of affairs—with the Tupamaros getting increasingly violent, and the forces deployed against them even more so—Ester could not see how two young people as committed to social justice as Emilia and Jorge could be protected from arrest.

Ester tried hard to focus on the positive. A wedding, even one under these conditions, was an event to be looked forward to, and Violeta too had good news—Elena was pregnant at last! She glowed with good health, and she and Violeta spent hours each day preparing for the baby. They made every item: diapers of the softest cotton, receiving blankets, caps, vests, booties, all in white or pale green since they didn't know whether the baby would be a boy or a girl.

In spite of the fact that both families wanted it, Emilia and Jorge were firm about not having a church service. Neither of them were practicing Catholics, nor did they want any of the pomp of a church wedding. A simple, civil ceremony was all their families could expect. They consented to a reception, so long as it was kept small, for relatives and close friends only.

On the wedding day, November 28, 1973, Ester and Violeta were standing on the curb outside Ester's house in their silk dresses and high heels waiting for a taxi when Jorge, her son-in-law to be, showed up wearing a shabby dark blue suit. Ester supposed that she should have been prepared for it, but she could not contain her frustration, thinking all the while how irresistible Jorge was with his radiant smile and glowing look of happiness. She was doing her best to make him more presentable by brushing his coat and straightening his tie when her eyes fell on his feet.

"For heaven's sake, Jorge, couldn't you at least have worn socks under your moccasins? Violeta, go and get a pair of my husband's." Ester's husband had been dead for several years, but his belongings still occupied the wardrobes and dressers, as if he might come back from a long trip at any moment. "Thank goodness I never throw anything away!" Ester searched in her handbag for the key to the front door and handed it to Violeta. "Dark blue socks! Not brown or black! Hurry! The taxi will be here any minute."

Violeta ran down the path to the front door and disappeared inside the house.

"I'm sorry, Ester," Jorge said.

"It's all right. It's all right. It's just that—"

Jorge put his arms around her. "You wanted a church wedding, with Emi all in white. I know. Even if we were the people for it, these aren't the times."

"I am the people for it! I didn't raise my only daughter to become a . . . more and more are being arrested every day!"

Jorge was trying to comfort her when the taxi pulled up and Emilia jumped out of the front seat where she had been discussing politics with the driver.

"Jorge," Violeta said, hurrying up with the socks, "do you have the rings?"

Jorge, smiling like a man in a trance, patted his breast pocket. He was looking at his bride as if she were attired from head to toe in satin, instead of a dark blue linen jacket and skirt almost as shabby as his own suit.

* * *

The only part of Ester's dream for her daughter that came close to being realized was that Emilia and Jorge lived near enough to come to her house every week for lunch. Suspecting that it might be the only full meal they had during the week, Ester began calling on them every day, always taking something to eat. She asked few questions about their political activities, but by now she knew enough to fear that it was only a matter of time before Jorge and Emilia were arrested. Under the laws pertaining to national security, it was no longer necessary to commit a crime in order to be arrested. Being suspected of associating with anyone the military considered dangerous to national security was sufficient to place one behind bars.

When Emilia became pregnant in July of 1974, Ester allowed herself to hope that it would lead to a change in the young couple's lifestyle. She was encouraged when Emi told her that she was thinking of leaving for Buenos Aires. Citizens of the five dictatorships surrounding Argentina continued to flee there in droves, little knowing that under Juan and Isabel Perón, the shelter they sought would soon prove more dangerous than any of the perilous places they were leaving behind.

"Going to Argentina feels like a betrayal, with three thousand in jail here." Emilia told her mother. "I'm not one of them only because I've been lucky."

"Perhaps you can petition for them from Argentina. You have to think of the baby now."

Emilia postponed making the move until October, when suddenly, on his way home from the university, Jorge was arrested. It took all of Ester's powers of persuasion to convince Emilia to leave Uruguay without delay. It was what Jorge would want, her mother told her, not only for Emilia, but for their child. Jorge's family, she assured her daughter, would not abandon Jorge, and neither would she. They would petition, they would hire lawyers, they would visit Jorge, but Emilia had to go before they arrested her as well.

Standing in line to board the ferry for Buenos Aires, Ester counted the minutes until she could put her daughter on the boat. Emilia was pale, she looked ill and exhausted. Ester doubted if Emilia had slept at all the night before. There were policemen everywhere and Ester watched in horror as one of them approached. Her hand closed tightly on Emilia's arm. She was considering making a run for it when the policeman touched his cap and smiled. He was concerned about Emilia's condition and her appearance and offered to take her to the head of the line, so she wouldn't have to stand any longer than necessary. Ester was so relieved she almost hugged him.

* * *

Ester and Violeta, joined now by Elena, continued meeting every month to knit, and Ester, not seeming at all rattled, told them that her house had been searched twice since Emilia's departure.

"What were they looking for?" Elena asked.

"I don't know. Books perhaps. Emi left a substantial library behind."

Since the military takeover of the university a year before, many books had been banned, including art books containing nude figures; the works of Sigmund Freud, which were considered pornographic; those of Pavlov because he was Russian; and the writings of Bertrand Russell for being "a Communist snob."

"Get rid of them, Ester," Violeta said. "Burn them!"

"I refuse to do any such thing," Ester said indignantly. "It would be a horrifying act, burning a book!" She couldn't find the words to describe what destroying those books would have meant to her. Ever since she could remember, books had been her teachers, her mentors, her trusted companions. Burning them would be like setting fire to her friends. "I've been giving them away. Every night I put five or six of them in a bag and go for a walk. When I see a house where I think, I don't know why, that they might read a book, or at least not throw it away, I leave one by the front door."

Violeta and Elena shook their heads sadly and knitted in silence for several minutes, knowing full well what it must be costing Ester to give away her and Emilia's most treasured possessions.

The phone rang, making them all jump. Violeta hurried to answer it. Elena and Ester knew at once from the joyous cry she gave that the call was from Carla. Violeta had not heard from her for months, and she was crying with joy when she hung up. Carla, she announced, was in Argentina, pregnant, and due to give birth in February of the new year. Given her circumstances, all three of them agreed that this was not exactly cause for celebration, but perhaps becoming parents would inspire both Carla and Fernando, and Emilia and Jorge, to abandon the political advocacy that was making their lives so dangerous. Both families could then settle down to worrying about everyday concerns, not guerrilla activities, overthrown governments, kidnappings, and murder.

When Carla's baby, Gabriel, was born in February of 1974, Violeta went to Buenos Aires to see her daughter and new grandson. Nothing appeared to have changed. Carla was staying with others who were also in hiding, and Gabriel had been born at home with the help of the gynecologist father of a friend. Violeta returned to Montevideo more worried than ever.

Elena and Antonio were also about to have their first son, and in striking contrast to his cousin, Andrés was born in a hospital surrounded by family and friends, and went home to a small, but comfortable and safe apartment to begin life with his parents.

* * *

Juan Perón's second reign lasted a mere nine months. His wife, Vice President Isabel Perón, assumed the Presidency after his death on July 1, 1974. *El Brujo* continued to share the presidential mansion with the new president, serving as her private secretary and keeping his ministerial post. His influence became pervasive, with the Triple A stepping up its paramilitary operations.

The dictatorships surrounding Argentina were growing increasingly confident of their mandate. They enjoyed the support of the United States for their efforts to prevent communism from gaining a foothold in Latin America. They were also aware that even Argentina, technically still a democracy, was really ruled by *el Brujo* whose ideology was similar to their own. Many of the various *junta* members were graduates of the School of the Americas and defended the network they proceeded to establish as a natural outcome of their mission. If, they maintained, the communists communicated with one another and formed coalitions, why shouldn't those who opposed them do the same?

The coalition that emerged between Brazil, Chile, Paraguay, Bolivia, Uruguay and Argentina would later be known as Operation Condor, a code name for the exchange and storage of intelligence data concerning so called leftists, communists and Marxists.

Operation Condor's first high profile target was former Chilean Defense Minister and Commander-in-Chief of the Chilean Army, Carlos Prats González, and his wife Sofía Cuthbert Chiarleoni, who had sought refuge in Buenos Aires after the fall of President Allende's government and the installation of General Augusto Pinochet's regime. Carlos Prats planned to travel to Europe, where he intended to organize other Chilean exiles, among them Bernardo Leighton Guzmán, former leader of the Christian Democratic Party and Chile's Minister of Education. Leighton's criticism of the dictatorship led to his exile.

On September 30, 1974, Carlos Prats and his wife Sofia were dining with friends in Buenos Aires when a bomb was placed under their car. Later that evening, they were killed instantly by the explosion.

Following the pattern they would adopt for future assassinations, Operation Condor partners covered their trail well. Police and the media reported that the killings were the result of disagreements between leftist leaders. Over a decade would pass before any charges were brought against Carlos and Sofía's killers.

* * *

Sara, Emilia, and Carla could hardly believe that they were together again. They remembered the hours they had spent as teenagers dreaming of what their professions would be, of who they would marry, of where they would live. Never had they imagined themselves living in Buenos Aires, with Sara now employed as an assembly worker in a factory, Emilia cleaning offices, and

Carla running a free pre-school for the poor families in her neighborhood. Carla provided housing for other exiles, while Sara and Emilia helped organize their meetings. They also published copies of articles about human rights violations in Uruguay that appeared in Latin American and other world newspapers. They understood the danger inherent in these activities and lived unobtrusively, trying to blend in with their surroundings and not draw attention to themselves.

Mauricio, his brother Gerardo, Fernando, and several other Uruguayans, formed the PVP—*Partido de la victoria del pueblo* (The People's Victory Party). They collaborated with the Argentine *Montoneros* (guerrillas) and focused on tracking the increasing number of people who seemed to be disappearing. While they could find no record or trace of them, their captors were far from invisible. They operated under cover of darkness, in teams that traveled in unmarked cars. It served their purposes to draw enough attention to themselves during a capture to terrorize the population. Captives were not transported to police headquarters, but to places called *chupaderos* (from the verb *chupar*, to suck), where people were literally sucked in, where no records were kept, charges made, or legal proceedings followed—and from which few emerged alive.

The *Montoneros* discovered that before his death in July of 1974, Perón had given foreign military intelligence services authority to arrest exiles living in Argentina, making it clear that the "final disposition" of these prisoners would be left entirely to the military representing the prisoner's country, a move that violated Argentina's laws regarding the protection of both legal and illegal immigrants.

By now, every time someone connected with the PVP was arrested, all PVP members moved. Sara changed houses and apartments over a dozen times in three years. Members of the group kept irregular hours and rarely went home without taking a roundabout route to ensure that they weren't being followed. They used only public telephones when communicating with one another and were guarded in their speech—careful of the differences in language usage which could give them away as foreigners. In Argentina, the bus was called the *colectivo,* not the *ómnibus; croissants* were *medialunas,* half-moons, and eyeglasses were called *anteojos,* not *lentes.* They kept few written notes. Agendas and address books were out of the question. All information was memorized.

In November of 1974, several Uruguayans went missing. They were accused of having made threats against Uruguayan President Juan Bordaberry and newly-minted Argentine President Isabel Perón. Among them was the first of seventeen Uruguayan children who would disappear in Buenos Aires, along with his parents. Sara, Emilia and Carla went to work attempting to find out whatever they could about Yolanda, Floreal, and their three-year-old son Amaral. All they were able to discover was that shortly after Floreal left his house to buy food, several men in civilian clothes broke in and took Yolanda and Amaral. No trace of any of them could be found.

The women made flyers and mailed them to human rights agencies in Europe. Sara assumed the additional task of creating dossiers about Uruguayans arrested in Argentina, keeping track of dates, occasional releases, emigrations, and disappearances. She was beginning to suspect that one day these records might be all that survived of her exiled countrymen and women.

On December 27, the police in Canelones, near Montevideo, were notified by people living in the area that several bodies lay along one of the local roads. Arriving on the scene, the police found three female and two male corpses bearing evidence of gunshot wounds, which were believed to be the cause of death.

They were dressed in clothing and shoes of Argentine make and carried both Argentine and Uruguayan cigarettes and matches. Among the bodies were Floreal and Yolanda.

Their families heard the news on the radio. In a state of shock, they went to the nearest police station from where they were taken to identify the bodies. The nightmare in which they would be trapped for the next eleven years had only just begun.

> "Yolanda," Ester wrote to Sara, "had been shot in the neck, but at first glance, no other injuries were apparent. Floreal's body on the other hand was covered in bruises, particularly his back, which was purple, as if he had hemorrhaged. I heard all this from Maricel, Floreal's sister. The people who first saw the bodies told her that they were naked, so we are all wondering who clothed them and why. Don't give Emi all these details! (Knowing her I am sure she will find out anyway.) At the funeral home Maricel was told that both of Yolanda's legs had been fractured. Maricel is in a terrible state, poor woman. No one can or will reveal how Floreal and Yolanda were transported to Uruguay, or—worst of all—whether little Amaral was with them. An acquaintance of Maricel's husband told them that he had heard of executions that took place at the local military barracks on December 19, about a week before the bodies were found.
>
> P.S. What is Carla thinking, getting pregnant again when things like this are happening?"

When Sara read about the executions, she wondered if it was possible that there was some connection between them and the fact that in distant Paris, at 10:30 on the morning of the same day, December 19, Uruguayan Colonel Ramón Trabal, serving as military attaché to England and France, had been shot six times in front of his house on the Avenue Poincaré. Prior to this assignment, Trabal had been Director of Information Services for Uruguay's National Defense Ministry. It was said that Trabal possessed tapes of the secret negotiations the military made with the Tupamaros at the time of British Ambassador Geoffrey Jackson's kidnapping and subsequent release. (Ambassador Geoffrey Jackson had been kidnapped on January 8, 1971 and was released on September 10 of the same year.)

Amaral's aunt Maricel knew nothing about Operation Condor, or what was happening in distant Paris. She was tormented with thoughts of her little nephew having been present at the barracks and witnessing the torture and death of his parents. Was it possible, Maricel wondered, that Amaral too had been killed? Hoping that by some remote chance Amaral might still be in Buenos Aires, Maricel and her husband Alberto traveled to the Uruguayan consulate there and hired a local lawyer to institute legal proceedings to find their nephew. Maricel and Alberto made the rounds of barracks and police headquarters. No matter where they turned, they met with the same response. There was no record of Floreal or Yolanda's arrest. Therefore the authorities could not answer the question of how they had turned up dead in Uruguay. They did not hesitate to imply that anything could happen to people who were involved with the guerrillas. As for Amaral, they recommended searching the orphanages.

Maricel and Alberto found the hours of darkness in Buenos Aires terrifying. Four or five people were killed openly every night, and an unknown number disappeared. The feeling of being in a surreal nightmare continued throughout their stay, culminating in a moment of sheer terror when, on the boat back to Montevideo, with no news of their nephew Amaral, and distraught with worry, they were confronted by Argentine marines who boarded the ship and took more than fifteen people away with them. Terrified that they might be next, none of the passengers or crew moved to intervene or protest. They sat still and silent, eyes darting from their feet up to the marines, waiting to see what would happen next.

A profound silence followed the marines' departure. Everyone wanted to believe that they were safe again, at least for a while. Could they have done anything, a few of them wondered? Protesting would only have got them arrested too. Some people crossed themselves. Others burst into tears. A few lit cigarettes with trembling fingers. Gradually, with sighs of relief, of shame, of hopelessness, they told one another that surely the others had been taken for a reason. They must have done something . . .

Maricel and Alberto clung to one another in a state of even greater anxiety than before.

* * *

Early in 1975 President Isabel Perón signed a secret decree authorizing the military to eliminate the guerrillas operating in the province of Tucumán. The military used it as a trial run for the system of controls they wished to impose on the entire country. The decree placed a limit on the amount of time prisoners could be held in isolation without charges being brought against them, but this turned out to be as farcical as the operation itself.

Led by General Acdel Edgardo Vilas—who believed that the fight was between his Forces of Light and the Kingdom of Darkness—five thousand Argentine soldiers were sent to face one hundred and fifty guerrillas.* The general later boasted that all the guerrillas had been captured without the loss of a single life on the part of his troops. He was proud of the fact that it was in Tucumán that the first clandestine detention center was established. It was named *La Escuelita*, The Little School, because it had once functioned this way. It was at *La Escuelita* that the practice of "hooding" began as well as the first experiments with electric

---

* Like General Vilas, US Attorney General John Ashcroft also saw himself as a rightful warrior. In a speech he delivered at Bob Jones University in 1999, Ashcroft shared his belief that a culture recognizing any king other than Jesus would "release Barabbas."

prods applied to the nipples, genitals, and gums. In another innovation, prisoners were buried for days up to the neck out of doors and hung from wires until their muscles lay exposed.

CHAPTER IV

I categorically deny that there exist in Argentina any concentration camps or prisoners being held in military establishments beyond the time absolutely necessary for the investigation of a person captured in an operation before they are transferred to a penal establishment.

ARMY COMMANDER JORGE RAFAEL VIDELA

* * *

Whomever the powerful dub an "evildoer," so may his rights be suspended or ignored.

WILLIAM F. SCHULZ, EXECUTIVE DIRECTOR (1994-2006),
AMNESTY INTERNATIONAL USA

V ioleta did not learn of the birth of Carla's second child for several days, but as soon as the news arrived, she went to Buenos Aires with Emilia's husband Jorge, who had been released on the condition that he leave Uruguay. Jorge was overjoyed at being with Emilia when their baby was born, and peppered Violeta with questions about labor, delivery, and the care of newborns. They were greeted at the dock by Emilia herself, in the full bloom of her pregnancy. For a long time she and Jorge clung to one another, weeping with joy and relief at being together again. Violeta waited patiently until Emilia pulled away from Jorge and hugged her. She had borrowed a car, Emilia said, and would take Violeta to Carla's.

As they drove through the city toward the poorer outskirts of town, Violeta became more and more concerned. Thank goodness her husband had stayed behind, she thought. Both of them came from humble backgrounds and had entered the middle class through hard work and determination, so Ramón would have been crushed to see that one of his children had returned to the kind of neighborhood and lifestyle he had spent his life putting behind him. *Don* Ramón felt it to be a personal failing that after working so hard to provide for his children, Carla seemed to be throwing his efforts in his face, speaking disdainfully of "bourgeois values;" laughing at her mother's habit of preserving the furniture by covering it with plastic, and ridiculing her father for always coming to the dinner table wearing a jacket.

Any hope Violeta might have had that they would keep driving until they left the slums behind ended when Emilia pulled up outside a three-story apartment building covered in graffiti. The steps crumbled beneath her feet as she entered what passed for the foyer, and the smells of frying fat made Violeta slightly nauseous as she climbed to the third floor.

Perhaps, she thought later, lying in her little hotel room, she would simply not tell *don* Ramón that she had found their daughter and grandchildren living in a slum. She suspected that he would also not want to hear how devoted Fernando was to them, how hard he worked, and how happy he and Carla seemed to be with the life they were leading.

Violeta bought clothes, food, and toys, and spent every waking moment with her family. Gabriel was barely a year old, and already he strung words together, could count to fourteen, and knew the first few letters of the alphabet. He was walking, and very protective of his newborn brother. The first time Violeta had approached Daniel's crib Gabriel stood by it and made it very clear that he did not want her to touch the baby. By the time she left, they had become fast friends, and Violeta had spent hours reading to him and taking him on the bus to a park where he could ride on the swings. She cried all the way back on the ferry, wishing she could have brought the babies home with her.

* * *

A month later on March 22, 1975, after a long night of labor, Jorge and Emilia's baby was born, weighing almost ten pounds. They named her Mariana. "She will walk the earth with feet of silver," Jorge said, and Emilia sang her favorite lullaby, *"Your laughter sets me free, gives me wings, takes loneliness away . . ."*

Ester rushed over to Buenos Aires to see her granddaughter. "There she was," she later told Violeta, "all white and pink, with those enormous gray-blue eyes that take up most of her face."

Mariana was a lively, intelligent, and beautiful baby, and both sets of grandparents came and went as often as they could to visit her. Emilia and Jorge were devoted to her, and regularly sent letters to Montevideo as if written by Mariana with news of her development.

> *"My mother tells me that I am growing disobedient because I do things I 'can't do.' I want to know, why can't I? Why, for instance, can't I open cupboard doors, take out pans and plates, investigate the fridge, etc? She doesn't understand that I am big now and I have a right to the whole house."*

Once Mariana could crawl, she went to spend the summer months with Ester in Montevideo, where she could enjoy the sun, the beach, and the fresh air. It took all of Ester's willpower to return her grandchild to the back streets of Buenos Aires and to the dangerous lifestyle her parents continued to lead.

"I know that you wanted me to become a teacher, like you," Emilia said as they packed Ester's overnight bag for the trip back to Montevideo.

"Or a lawyer. I was happy when you decided to study law."

"And now the future is so uncertain. But it's luminous, *mamá*, because it's based on solidarity, and on love! Not just Jorge's and my love for each other, but a reciprocal love between all people. I believe in people, in their capacity to struggle, to give of themselves, to build a better world for everyone."

"I know you do, *corazón*, it's one of the things that worries me most about you!"

"I don't regret anything, *mamá*; time and history will be with me and with all those who think as I do."

"If everyone felt that way, the world would really be a better place. But now there's Mariana to think about."

"She would reproach me all her life if I didn't sacrifice now to secure a better future for her."

"This isn't a very good neighborhood to be bringing up a child."

"It's just poor, *mamá*. Jorge says that there's nothing better than working, sharing, living with the people."

"His parents worry about him, too."

"They're always asking him if he's happy. But for Jorge and me happiness doesn't depend on whether we have more things, on whether work is easy or difficult, or our house better or worse than other people's. As long as we have enough to eat and live, that's enough for us. We're afraid sometimes too, like everyone else, but if we let fear rule us, then we deny our dreams."

* * *

Thousands of miles away in Rome, Bernardo Leighton Guzmán, the leader of Chile's Christian Democratic Party, was working to establish a coalition of the Christian Democratic Party and leftist political parties, and the return of democracy to Chile. Leighton had been permitted to leave Chile but forbidden from returning. General Augusto Pinochet's regime had charged him with fomenting anti-Chilean activities, but Leighton was undeterred.

On October 6, 1975, as Leighton approached his house, accompanied by his wife, he was shot in the forehead, the bullet exiting out of his left ear. His wife was shot in the chest. Both of them survived, she paralyzed, he scarred and with his hearing seriously impaired. For those who were by now tracking these deaths, it was no surprise that the next target was Bolivian General Joaquín Zenteno Anayo, an opponent of dictator Hugo Banzer. Zenteno Anayo was shot outside his embassy in Paris.

A meeting was held that year to formalize the agreement already in existence between Operation Condor partners Argentina, Brazil, Uruguay, Bolivia, Paraguay, and Chile. The heads of military intelligence of all six countries were in attendance, creating a data bank and a central information system with data about people they considered communist, leftist, socialist—or in any way opposed to the military's management of the fight against "subversion." Plans were made for the teams that would watch, detain, jail, and repatriate opponents of the regimes. The first phase of their operation would consist of exchanging information on the activities of the enemy. The second would be identifying *el blanco*—the target—and the third, the detention and transfer of said target to their country of origin. The exchange would be made directly between intelligence agencies, with the location to be determined at the time of capture.

* * *

Now that both Carla and Emilia were mothers, Sara often found herself fantasizing about having a baby. With all that she was learning about abductions, disappearances, torture, and murder, she wondered at this urge to conceive a child, and tried to keep the memory of the missing Amaral present. In one of her letters, Ester had related that recently in Montevideo an aunt of Amaral's had been approached by a Volkswagen while she was out walking.

> *The men in the car informed her that they knew where Amaral was and could show him to her. They persuaded her to get in the car, put a hood over her head, and drove her around for about an hour. When the car finally stopped, she was helped out, and the hood was removed. She was led to the window of a house and told that Amaral was inside, reading with other children. She looked in but was not at all certain that the child she saw was Amaral. On the way back, she was told that if they stopped causing trouble and appealing to the courts, Amaral's return could be arranged. She knew that this was just intimidation, but the family is keeping a low profile anyway while they wait for further news.*

What had happened to Yolanda and Floreal, Sara thought, could just as easily happen to her, Mauricio, and their child. It was madness to think of motherhood at such a time, but her period was already three weeks late. Without telling Mauricio, Sara went in for a pregnancy test. When her pregnancy was confirmed, she kept the news to herself, unsure about how Mauricio would react, and equally uncertain of her own feelings. She had no doubt that she wanted to have the baby, but at the same time her fear of what might befall them all was very real. She decided to talk it over with Carla and Emilia.

They met at a favorite little café near Carla's on a day when Jorge was home and able to take care of his own and Carla's children. They ordered coffee and hot ham and cheese sandwiches and exchanged the latest news about Amaral. The family had received a message that he would be turned over to them at his grandfather's gravesite.

"They waited for hours," Emilia said. "No one came."

"Bastards!" Carla said. "How can they play that way with people's feelings?"

"And then Amaral's Uncle Alberto got a call at work telling

him that his house was being overrun by police, soldiers, all in plain clothes. He said they held a gun to his mother and almost killed the dog."

"And they took all the clippings about the family's search for Amaral!"

"And Maricel!" said Emi.

"They took Maricel?" Sara gasped.

"They put her in a car," Carla said, "blindfolded her and drove her around—the usual. Then she was taken to a barracks and kept there all day. Then to a cell and in the end to an interrogation room where they finally took off her blindfold."

"Then they questioned her about 'the nephew she'd lost.'"

"'We didn't lose him,' Maricel told them. 'He disappeared!'"

"Good for her!" said Sara.

"Finally, they gave back her wedding ring and her identity card and drove her home."

"She was a nervous wreck, poor thing!" Emilia said. "Her daughter had been forced to sit in the living room while the gang searched the house. She's developed a stutter. She was terrified!"

"This is no time to have children, is it?" Sara said.

Carla and Emi exchanged a glance.

"Are you trying to tell us something, Sara?" Carla asked.

Sara nodded. She had expected her friends to be pleased. They both knew how much she wanted a child. But their smiles were sad, their congratulations forced. "You think I'm an idiot to have a baby now?"

"Well," Emi said, "we don't know what will happen, do we?"

"You two had children anyway!"

"It isn't that," Carla said. "We have to tell her, Emi."

"Tell me what?"

Mauricio, it appeared, had been seeing his former wife. Her friends had known about it for a couple of weeks but hadn't found the courage to tell Sara until now.

Sara got up from the table.

"Sara, we're so sorry!"

"I'm not angry at you. I just need to be alone."

* * *

Back at the apartment, before allowing herself any time to feel the pain she sensed was building in her like a wave, Sara packed her few belongings and was about to leave when Mauricio's brother Gerardo came to the door.

"So you found out?" he said, glancing at the suitcase. "Have you told him?"

"I haven't seen him."

"About the pregnancy, I mean."

"How do you know about that?"

"Next time you want to keep something a secret, don't go to one of our doctors."

"You didn't tell Mauricio, did you?"

"That's for you to do. I told the doctor to keep his mouth shut. But I think Mauricio has a right to know."

"Not anymore. I might have forgiven him if it had been some tramp or a casual affair. But the wife he swore he'd left?"

"You've always known what Mauricio is like where women are concerned. He's impulsive. But he does love you, Sara. He's talking about getting a divorce."

Sara laughed.

"Are you going to go through with the pregnancy?"

* * *

Sara moved in with Carla and Fernando, and every day a message came from Mauricio in the form of a note or a phone call. He stood at the corner and followed her to the bus stop, or waited for her when she left work, but Sara refused to speak to him. After a week, he gave up, and Sara began to look for an apartment. She returned to Carla's one evening, tired from walking from one part of the city to another, and discouraged by what was available on her small salary. Carla and Fernando were out, and on the table lay a large bunch of red carnations with an envelope attached to them. It contained a note from Mauricio and one from his lawyer in Montevideo, confirming that Mauricio's divorce papers had been filed. Sara moved back in with him, and he did his best to appear enthusiastic at the prospect of becoming a father.

Sara wondered at what makes men and women fall in love. What a time to entertain such thoughts, she told herself. Not only was she going to have a baby, but events were unfolding that threatened to make their current precarious existence seem secure by comparison.

* * *

Rumors reached President Isabel Perón that the military were planning a takeover but negotiations were still possible. She arranged a meeting with her ministers and the various heads of the armed forces for the morning of March 23, 1976 and left the Casa Rosada—Argentina's presidential house—to board the helicopter waiting to transfer her to her residence in Olivos. She had not been airborne long before the pilot, claiming a malfunction, landed the helicopter at an air force base four kilometers away, where the President was invited to drink coffee with the head of the base while the helicopter was repaired. A general, a brigadier, and an admiral were waiting to present her with a document announcing her resignation. She signed it, and proceeded to Bariloche, where she would see out the remainder of her presidency under house arrest. *El Brujo*, whom she had appointed Ambassador Extraordinaire to Spain, did not come to her rescue. He went into hiding and spent the next ten years evading justice.

On March 24, the Argentine Congress was dissolved and government buildings all over the country occupied by military personnel. It was the sixth time in half a century that a democratically elected government was overthrown in Argentina. Supreme Court justices were replaced, and the death penalty established for political crimes. Labor rights, including the right to strike, were immediately cancelled, union offices occupied, and their funds confiscated.

The *Junta*, led by General Jorge Rafael Videla, declared this to be the first battle of the Third World War.

With the fall of Argentina, Venezuela and Colombia became the only democracies left standing on the South American continent.

Just as in neighboring Uruguay, the military in Argentina had effectively dismantled the guerrillas first, and then assumed power, engaging in a highly effective campaign to convince people that the guerrillas were stronger than ever. Very few people knew how few the guerrillas in both countries were, and how frequently terrorist acts attributed to them had in fact been carried out by right wing groups under the protection of the military, such as the Triple A. In spite of the fate suffered by so many highly-placed military men who persisted against all odds in defending the constitutions of their various countries, retired Lieutenant Colonel Bernardo Alberte—who had already served time for his opposition to military interferences—wrote a letter to General Videla pointing out the illegality of recent events. He was promptly thrown from the sixth floor of his apartment building.

Considering such risks, it seemed almost incredible to Sara that certain groups of people refused to be silenced. Among them were the defense attorneys who took political cases and became favorite targets of the Triple A, and journalists who persisted in investigating and writing about events in spite of receiving threats, being arrested, held without charges, and ultimately disappearing.

A month after the *Junta* assumed power, Lieutenant Colonel Jorge Eduardo Gorleri, head of the fourteenth Regiment of the Airborne Infantry, invited journalists to witness a public burning of "pernicious literature which affects our intellect and our Christian way of being . . . and ultimately our most traditional spiritual ideals, encapsulated in the words God, Country and Home."

Close to one hundred writers would pay with their lives for authoring such literature. Some of them joked about the irony of having spent years, sometimes decades, striving to get published and be taken seriously as writers, only to find themselves suddenly taken so seriously, and considered so powerful and influential, that their books were banned and burned, and they were persecuted and imprisoned.

* * *

As April of 1976 drew to a close, the Río de la Plata began disgorging mutilated bodies onto the Uruguayan shores along Colonia and Rocha. The governing Security Council was quick to claim that they were not Uruguayan, but Asian. Stories were circulated of a mutiny aboard a fishing vessel, where in the way of uncivilized foreigners they had murdered each other and thrown the bodies overboard. Wounds were attributed to fish. It did not take the press long to uncover that the bodies all belonged to Uruguayans arrested in Buenos Aires earlier that year.

By May, Uruguay, with a population of three million, was housing seven thousand political prisoners, and 49 percent of its national budget was devoted to the Ministries of the Interior and Defense. The education budget had shrunk from 21 percent to

13.5 percent. It became more imperative than ever for the government to silence the voices that questioned the wisdom of spending more on the military than on education. Among those voices was that of Héctor Gutierrez Ruíz, President of Uruguay's House of Representatives until the military takeover, and former senator and Minister of Education, Zelmar Michelini. Both had moved to Argentina, where they had met with several of their countrymen to discuss holding elections in Uruguay.

On May 18 Gutierrez Ruíz was taken from his house, which his kidnappers sacked, and from which they stole seven suitcases containing the family's belongings. A few hours later, Zelmar Michelini, working at the time as a columnist for the newspaper *La Opinión*, was abducted from the Liberty Hotel in Buenos Aires.

Three days later their corpses were found, handcuffed and riddled with bullets, in an abandoned pickup along with the bodies of two of their friends. All four had been tortured.

* * *

Sara and Emilia sat in the park trying to absorb this news. By now, Sara thought, she should have become inured to horror. She had chosen the path of revolution, but somehow, events had spun out of control. It was one thing to confront soldiers and policemen; to destroy a few political targets; even, painful as it was, to accept the occasional accidental death of an innocent bystander. But the extent of the violence that had been unleashed against the revolutionaries was incomprehensible to her.

She looked at Mariana, a little over a year old, sitting in her pram, holding a small cloth book. She was a beautiful baby, with a perfectly round head, curly brown hair, and big blue-gray eyes.

"It's taken me all this time," Sara said, taking a colorful knitted hat with three pompons out of her bag, "but I finally made her something—with more love than skill!"

"I didn't know you could knit!" Emilia said.

"Your mother taught me when we were little."

Emilia put the hat on Mariana, whose serious expression made the hat look somehow incongruous. "Sometimes I think she's very old," Emilia said. "Older than I am. She looks at Jorge and me as if—" She hesitated.

"What, Emi?"

"I was going to say as if we're guilty of something. I've been wondering if it was wrong to have her, living as we do in this time . . ." She looked nervously around her, "in this place." Her eyes fell on Sara, who was seven months pregnant. "Sorry, Sara."

"I've had the same doubts."

"I used to think that if I didn't resist, my children would ask me why I hadn't fought for a better world for them."

"Do you regret it, Emi?"

"No. But now I know that the only world they care about is their own, the one that holds them and the people who love them. What can they understand about social justice and equality?"

"Remember that night when we were all so inspired by that speaker who said that when one dreams, one must give oneself to the bone?"

"And now it's real." Emilia took Mariana out of the pram and put her on her lap. "Sometimes I'm so frightened I can't get out of bed."

Sara put an arm around her. "The United Nations is helping people to leave."

Emilia shook her head. "Jorge won't go. He says there are others in more danger than we are and they have to go first."

"Go without him."

"I can't. He's as much a part of me as Mariana is."

"Send her to your mother."

"She went for six weeks last summer and I missed her so much

I thought I'd die! We've given Jorge's sister, Lucía, legal custody of Mariana. She's going to a nursery school near Lucía's work, and she spends every weekend with her. We call her every day at the same time. If three days go by and she doesn't hear from us, she'll know something's happened."

"Whenever people decide to go to war, contraceptives should be put in the water!"

They burst out laughing and Mariana studied them in her serious way.

"Look!" Sara said. "Carla is coming."

"She's so thin. I think having two babies in a row like that took everything out of her."

"I'm going to buy some *bizcochos!*" Sara said. "I'll be right back." She crossed the street to a bakery and came back with a paper bag full of little salty rolls and sweet croissants.

The three of them sat and ate, throwing the crumbs to the pigeons.

"Sara," Carla said, "I need visas for three more people."

"If they're for you and Fernando and the babies, the Refugee Committee has already told me they'll issue them. They think a lot of you, Carla. They know how many people you've housed."

"We couldn't leave our families," Carla looked away. "Think of my poor mother if I was living thousands of miles away."

"I despair of both of you!" Sara said, brushing crumbs from her lap.

"You're always telling us to leave, Sara," Emilia said. "What about you?"

"Until my baby is born my job is to take care of you!"

"Can you get the visas, Sara?"

"I'll ask. I promise."

"I have to go," Emilia said. "Jorge will be home soon. Thank you for Mariana's hat, Sara! I love it on her!"

"Be careful!"

"Always!"

Emilia tucked a blanket around Mariana's legs. When she reached the edge of the park she turned to wave. It was the last time Sara and Carla ever saw her.

* * *

When Sara got home, Mauricio was packing all of their political books, articles, and pamphlets. Sara did not need to be told what was happening. She took off her coat and went to work.

"Who was it this time?"

She was totally unprepared for the news that it was Mauricio's brother Gerardo who had disappeared. Mauricio looked deathly pale. It was like losing a terminally ill relative, he said. One knows they are dying and yet when they actually go it feels unexpected. It was miraculous that Gerardo had not been caught before. He had masterminded kidnappings, bombed military headquarters, and organized raids on arsenals and banks.

Sara offered to check all the hospitals, but Mauricio said that he would do that, and also report Gerardo's disappearance to the United Nations High Commission for Refugees. Sara should finish packing all the incriminating materials and move them to the home of their friends, the Juliens. Roger Julien was a French citizen and they all hoped that would offer him the kind of protection none of the others could hope for.

Mauricio's search of the hospitals turned up nothing, and he and Sara spent several sleepless nights, expecting the door to be broken down at any moment. On the third day, Mauricio was summoned to a meeting of his guerrilla unit. One of the members, Washington Pérez, had a story to tell and a message to deliver. Several armed men had broken into his apartment in the dawn hours, and instead of beating him up and stealing his belongings as was the norm, he had been instructed to accompany them on a visit to see a friend. He was hooded, put into a car, and driven around for half an hour. When the car stopped he heard the words "Open Sesame" and the sounds of a garage door opening. He was helped up some stairs and when his hood was removed, found himself sitting in a small room containing a safe and a desk. On the desk was a photo of Adolf Hitler. Behind the desk sat a middle-aged man he recognized as the notorious Triple A member Aníbal Gordon. Standing by his side was an Uruguayan Army Major who didn't hesitate to identify himself as Nino Gavazzo.

It was explained to Pérez that in exchange for freeing Gerardo and ten others, Gavazzo and Gordon wanted ten million dollars, and the return of the flag.

"What flag?" Pérez asked.

"The one the ERP stole from the military museum at the Cerro. It's part of our national patrimony."

"The flag I may be able to manage. But how am I supposed to find ten million dollars?"

"Ask those so-called human rights agencies, the ones that are taking such an interest in our affairs."

Pérez very much doubted that he could raise even a tenth of the amount they were demanding but stalled by saying that he would have to see Gerardo first to confirm that he was still alive.

"The Federal Police have tortured him rather brutally," Gavazzo said.

Pérez laughed mirthlessly to himself as he was hooded again and taken down two flights of stairs. He had no particular affection for the Federal Police, but knew only too well that if Gerardo had been tortured, it was much more likely that it was Gordon and Gavazzo who had done it.

It was a cold night and the more steps he descended the more frigid the air felt. He heard a door being opened and was asked to step forward. His hood was removed and the door closed behind him. What little light there was in the room came from a dim, bare bulb hanging on a cord from the ceiling. At first, Pérez wasn't sure what the piles of rags were that covered the floor, but then some of them shifted and moved, and the stench that hit his nostrils made him gag. He fumbled in his pocket for a handkerchief to cover his nose and mouth, and nearly jumped out of his skin when he felt a touch on his leg and saw that one of the rag piles was reaching for him.

Recognizing Gerardo, Pérez squatted next to him, not knowing whether to touch him or not. He was covered in wounds, all of which looked infected, and his eyes were inflamed. As Pérez's vision adjusted to the dim light, he saw that Gerardo's left side was paralyzed. It was obvious that he had had a stroke.

"What have they done to you, man?" Pérez said, removing his coat and trying to wrap Gerardo in it.

"No," Gerardo whispered, "no. It'll be worse afterwards." His words were slurred and Pérez could barely understand what he was saying.

"Where the hell are we?" Pérez asked.

"Automotores Orletti. Gordon's playground."

"They want ten million dollars for you. And the flag."

"What flag?"

"The one the ERP stole from the Cerro."

Gerardo laughed and had a coughing fit Pérez thought might be the end of him.

"They're all murderers," he whispered as soon as he could talk again, "don't make any deals. And don't give them the fucking flag!"

* * *

"She didn't eat her spinach," Jorge said, looking at Mariana's plate.

Emilia jumped up. "I'll get her hat."

"What?"

"The hat Sara made her," Emilia said. "She'll eat anything when she has it on."

Jorge laughed.

"Don't laugh, it's true! Look!" She put the hat on Mariana and offered her a spoonful of spinach. Mariana took it and opened her mouth for more. Jorge was still laughing when he heard the sounds of a car pulling up outside. He looked out cautiously and dropped the curtain, jumping up from the table.

"Let's go!"

Emilia needed no prompting. She picked Mariana up and ran for the back door, followed by Jorge. They had almost reached it when both the front and back doors came crashing in. Heavily armed men in civilian clothing surrounded them and wrestled Jorge to the ground, cuffing his hands behind him and covering his head with a dark hood.

Little Mariana was taken from Emilia by a man in dark glasses and a leather jacket and carried into the kitchen while Emi was also cuffed and hooded. Lying on the floor, unable to see, Emi struggled to hear over the shouts of the men. Mariana had not cried, and as the men scattered to search the house, she heard the leather-jacketed man saying, "Why would anyone put an ugly hat like this on such a beautiful baby?"

* * *

Carla and Fernando were lying in their bed, keeping one another warm. Gabriel, their eighteen-month-old, and Daniel, the baby, were asleep in a crib.

Two cars drove down the dark street below their windows and six armed men in civilian clothing got out, their breath misting in the cold pre-dawn air as they glanced quickly around. Windows were closed, blinds and curtains drawn. Even if anyone was awake to see them, no one would dare to intervene.

"Every time I make love to you," Fernando said, "it's like the first time."

"Better, I think!" Carla laughed, snuggling her back up against his chest.

The sounds of footsteps in the corridor outside their apartment woke Gabriel with a start and he sat up, calling for his mother. Just as Carla reached him, the front door was broken down. As Fernando jumped out of bed, reaching for his pants, both babies began to cry.

* * *

Concerned that Jorge's sister Lucía might not have heard the news about her brother, Sara dialed Ester's number in Montevideo. Her hands were shaking.

"Hello."

Hearing Ester's voice, Sara was struck momentarily dumb.

"Hello! Who is it?"

"Ester. It's Sara."

She did not have to say another word. Ester knew what the call meant.

"Both of them?" she asked.

"And Mariana."

"No!"

"Ester, can you call Violeta?"

"Carla is gone too?"

"And Fernando. And the children."

"All gone?"

"All of them."

* * *

105

Ester tried to quell the feeling of nausea she felt as she buttoned her long wool coat and prepared to meet Violeta at the ferry. How had it come to this? How was it possible that two respectable families wanting only that their children graduate with honors and find good marriage partners, were now faced with the reality of those children in jail and their grandchildren disappeared?

Violeta thought that her husband would have a seizure when she broke the news to him. He began to shake and his face turned purple. Then he said he would go with her. Violeta talked him out of it. He would have to be taken care of and she didn't want the responsibility. She and Ester understood what needed to be done and would work as a single force. She persuaded him that he needed to stay behind and rally the family for the work ahead of them.

The wind blew cold off the river as the two women disembarked in Buenos Aires a few hours later and left the dock to find a taxi. They gave the driver Emilia and Jorge's address and rode in silence; one never knew who was an informer and how words could be used against one these days. They paid the driver at the curb and approached the little house with a window on the street. No effort had been made to repair the broken-down front door. Its shattered remains listed precariously, shards of wood pointing like spears toward the sky. They moved some pieces aside and stepped into the small living area. Nothing of any value or use was left in the house. Every scrap of clothing had been taken, every book, every plate and pot. A broken chair lay on the floor, along with some newspapers and a fork with twisted tines. The kitchen was bare of appliances, the only item a piece of colored wool in a corner. Ester picked it up. It was a little cap, with three pompons on the top. Ester put it in her pocket, and she and Violeta continued the search. They opened every cabinet, searched every closet, but there was nothing there.

A similar scenario awaited them nearby at Carla and Fernando's. Only there, thanks to the neighbors who had run into the apartment as soon as the gang had left, collecting everything they could find, there were two invaluable items—the little boys' birth certificates. Unlike Emilia and Jorge's neighbors, who had not answered their doorbells, these neighbors were willing to tell Violeta that Carla and Fernando had been taken during the night and the children left in a neighbor's care. A woman stepped forward, clearly wishing she did not have to. "I kept them for two days. The baby cried all the time! I couldn't calm him. My husband said he was going crazy and our own children were being neglected. I'm sorry, *señora*, but I gave them to the police."

* * *

"What do you mean you don't know?" Ester shouted at the policeman, brandishing Mariana's hat in his face.

"What kind of police force is this?" Violeta added. "Everything in our daughters' houses has been stolen or destroyed!"

"Where are they? Where are their husbands? Where are our grandchildren?"

The policeman held up his hands. "Perhaps they moved, *señoras.*"

"Are you a complete idiot?" Ester said.

"Why would they break everything they owned before moving?"

"Some people—"

"You're playing us for fools," Ester said. "Murder has been done!"

"Children have disappeared!"

"*Señoras,* these are difficult times—"

"We know that the children were handed over to you!"

"Even if they were, we wouldn't have kept them, *señoras*. Try social services."

Social services did not know, or would not reveal, what had been done with them.

"We're mad, Violeta," Ester said as they sat warming their hands over cups of coffee. "We must be mad. How can such things happen?"

* * *

"The only thing we can do is search the orphanages," Sara told them. "I have a list, and I've borrowed a car."

They began in Buenos Aires. Violeta and Ester, accompanied by a nurse, walked along a row of cribs and playpens full of babies and toddlers. Some were crying, some lay in their cribs staring at the ceiling, some looked like miniatures of the shell-shocked soldiers they had seen on news reels after the Second World War.

"These were all brought in during the last few days," the nurse said.

Violeta and Ester smiled at the children, holding tightly to one another, afraid that if they let go they would break into a thousand pieces.

At the second orphanage they again reviewed a row of cribs and looked into a room full of one-to-three-year-olds. A few held their arms out to them, and it was all the two women could do to keep walking, to keep looking. Two babies had died, the nurse said, did they want to see the bodies? They had not prepared themselves for such an eventuality, but not confirming whether the bodies belonged to their grandchildren was not an option. They looked at one another and Ester nodded.

Once outside after viewing the bodies, they gave vent to every emotion that had racked them during their visit. They supported each other and sobbed until it seemed as if there were no more tears left in them. Then they blew their noses and told Sara that they were ready to continue.

They left Buenos Aires and began in La Plata.

Accompanied by a young doctor in a white lab coat, Violeta and Ester once more began the rounds, cradle by cradle, little face by little face. This was their last stop. If Mariana, Daniel, and Gabriel were not here, there were no more orphanages to search.

Suddenly, Violeta stopped in front of a crib containing a three-to-four-month old baby. There was an I.V. connected to the top of his head.

"Boy or girl?" Violeta asked.

"A boy. He's lost his suction reflex," the doctor said, caressing the baby's cheek.

"Let me see his left hand."

The doctor uncovered the baby's hand, revealing a small dark birthmark shaped like a crescent moon on the inside of his wrist.

"I need to sit down!"

The doctor hurried to bring a chair and Ester eased Violeta into it.

"It's him! I had to be sure. He was as fat as butter when he was born!"

"And will be again!" Ester said. "Where is his brother?"

"With the other two-year-olds."

"Please bring him!"

The doctor nodded. Before she left, she asked Violeta if she wanted to hold the baby.

"May I?"

"It's what these children need most." She disconnected the I.V., put Daniel in Violeta's arms and hurried away.

Daniel barely stirred. "He's dying!" Violeta cried.

"We'll make him well, you'll see! It's as the doctor said, he needs to be held."

They looked up as the doctor returned, carrying Gabriel. He did not look emaciated as his brother did, but his eyes were distant, vacant, and when his grandmother handed Daniel to Ester and took Gabriel in her arms, he did not respond.

"What do we have to do to claim them?" Ester asked the doctor.

"Take them."

"What? Just like that?"

"*Señora,*" the weary young doctor said, "follow my advice. If any questions are asked, I'll make something up. Everyone here is aware of what's going on with these children. I'm going to leave you now, to get a drink of water for your friend who nearly fainted. When I come back, perhaps the four of you will have found that side door over there and you'll be gone."

* * *

Sara was overjoyed and incredulous to see them emerging from the side of the building, each carrying a child. Her joy did not last long.

"Daniel is dying!" Violeta said. "I have to get him to a doctor."

"Not here!" Ester said. "In Montevideo!"

"How?" Sara asked.

"We'll think of a way! Hurry! Drive us to the ferry!"

By the time they reached the dock, they had worked out a plan. They knew that they would not be allowed to leave Argentina or enter Uruguay without documents stating that both parents had granted the children permission to travel. The laws in both countries were strict where this was concerned, an ironic circumstance that was not lost on the three women, who had until recently supported the farsighted legislators who had drafted them.

Sara parked the car, and Ester and Violeta went in to buy their tickets while she stayed with the children. As she held Daniel, Sara experienced a moment of sheer panic. What if her child was taken, just as Carla's and Emi's had been? She should have forgotten all about her desire to be a mother and never expose a child to the fate that had befallen these. No baby should have to suffer this way, she thought, looking at Daniel's gray skin, his tiny puckered hands, and the bones that showed starkly on his skull. And his brother, his serious, still, brother who was staring straight ahead and had not made a sound since he had been put in the car.

As had been arranged, Sara took the children and went into the terminal, making her way to the bathroom. There was a woman there washing her hands and Sara saw that two of the stalls were occupied. She waited until the woman had left and looked cautiously under the doors. Violeta and Ester were there.

What followed would have been comical if the situation was not so dire. She handed Gabriel to Ester and took baby Daniel into the stall where Violeta was waiting. Violeta was a substantial woman of generous proportions and the stall was narrow, making it difficult for her to maneuver around Sara to take off her jacket and hang it over the door. Using Sara's scarf, they tied Daniel to her chest, positioning him so he could breathe. Violeta then put her jacket back on and buttoned it over him. Having concealed the baby, they left the stall and placed the silent Gabriel in front of Ester, covering him with her long, full coat.

Before leaving the bathroom, Ester reached into her bag and took out Mariana's tiny hat. "You won't stop looking?" she asked, pressing it into Sara's hands.

"Never!"

When the three women emerged, Gabriel was walking just as he had been told, under Ester's coat and between her legs. Sara did not think they would get away with it. Long as the coat was, anyone looking closely would see his feet.

Supporting Ester as if she were very frail, Sara and Violeta made their way toward the counter where their tickets and documents would be examined. This, Sara thought, was surely the moment when one or both of the children would decide to cry.

"Take very good care of yourself, *mamá!*" Sara said loudly. "We don't want another attack! Sit down the minute you're on the ferry!"

The official appeared oblivious to them and to Sara's theatrics. He stamped their documents, returned their tickets and moved on to the next person in line.

They had done it! Sara thought. They were through Argentine customs.

* * *

Later that evening, Elena and Antonio opened the door to their apartment and found Violeta and Ester, each holding a baby.

"How you managed it," Elena said when the whole family gathered to see the children, "I don't know. On the boat, with the kids hidden in your clothes!"

Everyone was lost in admiration of what the two women had done.

"Such fortitude!"

"Such love!"

"Impossible without love."

"What you did was extraordinary!"

At the family council that followed, it was agreed that several of them would leave for Buenos Aires at once in an effort to find Carla and Fernando. As for the babies, the grandmothers each offered to take one. Antonio and Elena felt strongly that it was best not to separate the boys. Even though Elena was pregnant again, their argument that the boys had been through enough, prevailed.

It was an insane gesture, but Antonio and Elena could see no other solution. Placing the children with Josefina and Sergio was out of the question. Angry as they all were with Carla and Fernando for the family crisis, their disappearance made everyone all the more aware of how incongruous it would be to put their children into a military home. As for Fernando's mother, she was in poor health, and at the moment both she and Violeta had to deal with the fact that their own adult children were now among the disappeared.

The magnitude of what they had undertaken hit Elena and Antonio as soon as the door closed on the departing family.

"Look at him, Antonio," Elena said, her eyes on Gabriel. "One year old, and he has that hard look, as if nothing can reach him."

"He's wrapped in defenses," Antonio said. "I don't think he wants to see us."

"His eyes look lost."

"He's in shock, poor thing."

"But he's holding his head up, with that hard look."

As for Daniel, he was, as Antonio put it "a ruin." It was too risky to have Carla's children attended to at a medical facility. Any association with someone accused of being a *sedicioso*—a seditious person— could bring the military to the door.* They decided to ask Paco, a cousin of Antonio's who was a pediatrician, to examine Daniel. He lived miles from Montevideo, but there was no other solution. Antonio called him and Paco agreed to leave on the next available bus, which would bring him to the city by noon the following day.

That first night was a taste of what was in store for them. Antonio sat watching Daniel, who hardly seemed to be breathing. Every so often, Antonio put the nipple of a baby bottle to his lips, but Daniel didn't move. Sometimes he opened his eyes, staring into space.

---

* In September of 2020 Attorney General William Barr recommended that Black Lives Matter protestors should be charged with sedition, a charge usually brought against those conspiring to overthrow a government or start a war against their country.

Elena fed their son Andrés and put him to bed.

At around ten o'clock, Gabriel, who had been totally silent, began to scream. He cried, drooled and vomited the milk and bread he had eaten earlier that evening, and then began throwing himself at the walls. Andrés woke up, frightened and upset, and also began to cry. Antonio soothed his son, while Elena tried to calm Gabriel. Touching Gabriel only seemed to make him worse, but Elena had to protect him from hurting himself. She tore the bedclothes off the beds, collected pillows and cushions and put them and the mattresses against the walls. Gabriel's fit lasted over an hour, and by then Elena and Antonio were in a state of emotional exhaustion. When Gabriel fell asleep on the floor, they were afraid that he would wake and start screaming again, so they decided to leave him where he was with a blanket over him. Elena wiped up the vomit and put her son back in his crib while Antonio tried to get a few hours of sleep before leaving for work. Every half hour, Elena got up to see if Daniel was still breathing.

In the morning, the baby's skin was grayer and wrinkled and seemed to hang more loosely on his bones. He was shrinking before their eyes.

Gabriel was silent again. He simply sat on the floor watching Elena and his little cousin Andrés, and eventually was coaxed into eating the mashed potatoes and pumpkin she put before him.

Elena tidied up the house and waited for Antonio, who always came home for lunch and a siesta before going to his classes in the afternoon. Antonio had hardly taken a bite of his steak when the doorbell rang.

It was Paco. He was a large man, and the baby looked tinier than ever in his hands. When he had finished his exam, he said nothing for quite some time. Then he reached for a small suitcase. "He's seriously dehydrated and has lost his suction reflex. I'm going to start an intra-venous drip and show you how to keep it going. But I don't want to lie to you. You need to prepare yourselves for the fact that he might not live. It all depends on whether he responds to the hydration and decides to eat."

"What shall we give him?" Elena asked.

"Formula. I brought a sample. Make sure to mix it with boiled water only."

Elena went into the kitchen to prepare some at once while Antonio told Paco about their night with Gabriel.

"I've heard," Paco said, "that these children are sometimes given tranquilizers. I could have his blood tested, but I don't want to subject him to that. If it is the tranquilizers, the effect will wear off in a few days at most—he's experiencing withdrawal, especially at night, which is when he would have been sedated." Gabriel was studying him as if he understood every word. "He can't tell us what he saw, but he remembers it, and he's missing his mother."

The week that followed was horrendous. Gabriel stopped throwing himself at the walls, but every night at ten he woke with night terrors and screamed until well past midnight. Daniel surprised them by recovering his suction reflex within forty-eight hours, but as soon as he started eating, he also started crying. He would stop only when Elena walked him. Whenever his cousins cried, Andrés joined in. Elena tried to keep all three babies quiet so that Antonio could sleep for at least a few hours in order to be able to work and study, but it proved impossible. When her father-in-law came to see her a few days after Paco's visit, he was shocked by her appearance. Always slender, Elena was now gaunt and disheveled with dark shadows under her eyes. It was impossible, she told him, to find time to do anything except change diapers, wash diapers, and prepare food for the five of them. *Don* Ramón stayed all of that night and many that followed. In spite of the fact that Gabriel at eighteen months was already the spitting image of his father (who *don* Ramón blamed for all their troubles) the desperate condition of his two grandsons brought out the tenderest feelings in him, and he walked the floor all night with the children in his arms, relieving Elena as much as he could. She was growing increasingly worried that the baby she was carrying wouldn't develop normally under these conditions. She told her father-in-law that she was losing weight, barely slept, and her nerves were at snapping point. She would not have thought it possible to feel so exhausted and still be able to function. When the time came to go to the hospital she almost prayed for complications that would keep her there for weeks, sleeping for days on end. The birth, however, was uneventful and the new baby, Ricardo, was in extremely good health, and very calm, which was a blessing, since Elena now had four children, all in diapers.

She had dreamt about being called mother, and when her eldest, Andrés, began to say *mamá,* Gabriel copied him.

"No, Gabriel, I am not your mother. I am your aunt. Your mother is *Mamá* Carla, I am tía Elena."

Gabriel dutifully called her tía Elena, and soon her son Andrés did too.

"To them they're all brothers," Antonio said.

"I didn't go through everything I did to become pregnant only to have my own son call me aunt," she said to Antonio. "I told them all to call me *mamá.* We'll fix it later." But she worried about doing things right. Carla and Fernando would surely be found, and then she'd have to part with the boys. "I keep wondering what I can do to make it less devastating," she said, watching Andrés and Gabriel splashing in the tub while the two babies slept toe to toe in Andrés's old crib.

Antonio nodded.

"You seem worried," Elena said. She was sitting on a stool by the bathtub, enjoying a moment of unusual calm.

"I'm being followed," Antonio said.

"By whom?"

"A man, in plain clothes."

"You're sure?"

Antonio was certain. He was proved right the next day when they had to submit to a search of their apartment. So many uniformed men came through the door that Antonio was sure they wouldn't fit in the small room. They dumped their guns on the bed and began to search every cupboard, every drawer. Antonio counted thirteen weapons, the one pointing at them making fourteen. He and Elena sat in the living room trying to soothe Gabriel, who, as soon as he saw the guns, began to scream. His cousin Andrés joined him. Andrés's crying was imitative, it had none of the raw terror of Gabriel's screams, but it soon set the babies going as well. The crying concerned the soldiers searching the apartment, and several of them tried to intervene, making faces at the babies, offering them keys to play with.

"You're so young to have all these children!" one of them said to Elena. "Couldn't you space them out a little?" He turned to Antonio. "You should be more considerate. All this childbearing will kill your poor wife."

"What will kill my wife is the stress of having you here! Can you speed it up?"

When the soldiers left, Antonio and Elena laughed for the first time in a long while.

CHAPTER V

* * *

It would be inadmissible for the Argentine government to allow a foreign country to install a base of operations within its territory. Or, as has been alleged, to move about the cities carrying out armed operations, arresting people and finally putting them on a plane, taking them out of the country and to Uruguayan territory in the best of cases. And in others, killing them on Argentine territory. Fantasies such as these can only come from the mind of a novelist.

MAJOR JOSÉ NINO GAVAZZO, REGARDING THE RUMORS THAT URUGUAY AND ARGENTINA WERE COLLABORATING IN THE MURDER OF POLITICAL PRISONERS.

"This is a heroic thing you are doing, Elena," Violeta told her when she came to deliver the diapers she had made from old sheets.

"I don't feel heroic. I feel tired and grouchy. I feel cheated."

"Cheated? How?"

"All I wanted was to have a home and children. But I can't

devote time to any of them! No sooner do I have one cleaned up than another one poops, or throws up, or spills something. And the whole apartment smells of ammonia because Gabriel still has diarrhea and I have to boil the diapers. Do you know what they call me in the neighborhood? Our Lady of the Diapers!" Having started, Elena couldn't stop. "Gabriel was sitting on the bidet last week while I found a towel to dry him and Andrés opened the hot water tap and burned Gabriel badly. Not only did the poor little thing already have a rash from his diarrhea, now he's burned as well. When my relatives found out, all hell broke loose."

They had all been so worried and distressed about finding Carla and Fernando, Violeta realized, that they had neglected the situation developing right under their noses. "We've been very thoughtless. Why didn't you call me?"

"I don't have time! Sometimes I fall asleep on the toilet."

Violeta soon had a group of aunts and cousins each willing to devote a day a week to washing diapers, babysitting, and grocery shopping. Things got a little better for Elena after that, but she could not entirely get over her resentment. Nothing about marriage or motherhood had met her expectations. She must be a very shallow and naïve person, she told herself. First she'd believed that after the honeymoon she would move into a pretty little apartment, with a nice kitchen where she could try out her recipes from the Crandon cookbook her own mother had used and which had never failed her. Then she had assumed that she would get pregnant immediately and that the baby would only add to their happiness. Instead, Antonio had had little time to enjoy the meals she prepared, and rarely noticed if she made new curtains or put flowers on the table. It was all he could do to keep the job that supported them and put in the hours of classes and study required for his engineering degree. Elena too had worked, as a part-time teacher, telling herself that she would soon have a baby to fill in the hours while Antonio was gone. When she didn't get pregnant, everyone said not to worry, to enjoy the time before the responsibilities of parenthood changed their lives forever. The months had stretched into years and still there had been no sign of a baby. She had consulted several doctors. None could find anything physically wrong. She began to wonder if perhaps there was something wrong with Antonio but didn't want to suggest it. She counted the days around her periods obsessively, making sure that everything was auspicious on her most fertile days. And suddenly, with no consciousness of having done anything differently, she had conceived. The joy of it had been so intense that Elena could not help smiling at herself in every plate glass window she passed. She was pregnant! She was going to be a mother! Andrés's birth was difficult, but she got through it bravely, and before she knew it, she was pregnant again. And then the nightmare began. Whatever had possessed her to think that she could care for four children? The same instinct that had made her want so desperately to be a mother, she supposed. Gabriel's baby face frozen in fear and hurt, and Daniel unconscious in Violeta's arms had helped her to decide. She would save them! She would love away the hurt and the fear and feed Gabriel until he was once more as fat as butter. They would all play and laugh together and be a happy family. She had not counted on the trauma of what had happened to her nephews, on the physical and emotional wounds that healed, but very gradually. She loved them, but it was difficult to feel love when they were all demanding something from her and she couldn't even shower in peace, scrubbing and scrubbing with the nail brush until her skin was raw, and still, when she put her fingers to her nose, there it was—the faint smell of excrement. Her hands were red from being in water all day long, her nails cut to the quick, no longer the well-manicured hands she had been so proud of. She couldn't remember what it was like to sleep for more than two hours at a time, and sleep had become her only fantasy. She would have done anything to have one uninterrupted night of it. She imagined herself winning the lottery and hiring a nanny, or in her darker moments, slipping something into the babies' bottles so that she could have a few hours of peace and quiet. Her life consisted of nothing but drudgery, and she was starting to hate Antonio, who could leave for work or for the university and still enjoy some semblance of a social life. When was the last time she had met her friends for tea on the Rambla? Or gone to a movie? Or danced? She couldn't remember. The worst thing was the feeling that whatever she did was insufficient. She was sincerely trying to do her best by them, but if she sat down to play with one or give one a bottle, there was always another one crying, the sound cutting through her until she thought her head would split open, spilling all her vile thoughts onto the ground for the world to see. And who was to blame for all this misery? Carla and Fernando and their irresponsibility! If they couldn't look after children, if their life was incompatible with having babies, why had they done it? Now here she was paying the price. And she wasn't the only one. Violeta and Fernando's mother did not rest either. They went to human rights agencies, they visited the United Nations, and lobbied every government official they could reach, trying to find their children.

Their efforts eventually paid off. Carla and Fernando's files were located, and their family at last informed that Carla was being held at a prison in La Plata.

Elena thought she really would go mad then. Antonio's sister Josefina, Violeta, *don* Ramón, all of Carla and Antonio's family were relieved, ecstatic, talking of nothing else. No one seemed to notice her, or to consider what the news meant to her. She would have to give the two little nephews she had come to love as her own back to Carla. If only she had loved them less. If only her heart had not broken when she saw them that day at her front door, and if only it had not grown around them until they were as dear to her as her own babies.

Antonio couldn't understand why she was so angry, why she didn't join in the celebrations. Wasn't she glad that his sister was alive? Elena couldn't honestly answer that question. Her feelings for Carla were a tangled emotional web. No such confusion existed where Carla's children were concerned. She loved them as she did her own two boys and knew exactly what she would have wanted Carla to do for her if their situations were reversed.

Soon after they heard the news that Carla was alive, Antonio came home to find Elena waiting for him with an official looking form on the table between them. It was a request to be presented in Juvenile Court for a permit to travel with their two nephews to Buenos Aires.

"Are you out of your mind?" Antonio said. "They'll ask for documentation, they'll find out that the boys are here illegally. All of us could be arrested!"

"They won't ask. And we won't be arrested. Sergio will see to it."

Antonio sat down and put his head in his hands. "I don't want to be in his debt."

"Nor do I. But the boys should see their mother, and the sooner I get used to giving them up, the better."

The permit was issued, and since they had no money to pay for hotels, Antonio and Elena bought tickets for all six of them on the night ferry. They slept on the ship's deck.

From Buenos Aires they went to the prison at La Plata by train, changing diapers all the way.

When Antonio and Elena walked in with the four children Carla tried not to cry but Elena saw a fear and vulnerability in her that she had not been there before. It didn't last long. She was soon the same defiant Carla, interested only in her own two boys. Elena took her children and left Antonio with his sister. She had not received one word of thanks or acknowledgement for all she'd done, and later Antonio admitted reluctantly that neither had he.

* * *

Sara, now several months pregnant, kept hoping that now that Carla and Fernando had been found, news of Emilia, Jorge, and little Mariana would also surface. Sara haunted the United Nations offices, wrote letters to foreign papers, collected every fragment of evidence she could find about Emilia and her little family, and indulged in wild fantasies. She would somehow find out where they were being held and get them out! They would free Gerardo and take on the whole country! In calmer moments, she would laugh at herself. Wasn't that how this had all begun, with their desire to save the world? How did one deal with the abduction of friends, with the knowledge that Gerardo lay half dead in some hell-hole, and meanwhile give birth to a child who could suffer the fate of Carla's children, or worse, disappear like Mariana, without a trace? The decision not to terminate her pregnancy now seemed like the most selfish she had ever made. What kind of a mother would expose her child to such threats and dangers?

Mauricio meanwhile was busy negotiating a deal for his brother's release. He was torn between wanting to do whatever it took to free Gerardo, and the arguments of the other guerrillas, who maintained that Gerardo stood the same chance of coming out alive with or without a ransom. The only thing that might prevent Gerardo from being killed was international pressure and that was already being arranged.

With the same efficiency and single-mindedness with which she confronted all of her endeavors, when her labor began Sara took herself to the hospital and gave birth in a few short hours to a red-headed baby she named Simón. Everyone had told Sara to prepare for a long and painful delivery. She was having her first child and she was not as young as she used to be. But it wasn't a biological clock Sara was racing, it was time itself. She might not survive for much longer, her child might disappear, and every moment was of the essence.

When the time came to register their son's birth, Mauricio wanted to be listed as the father. Considering the recent kidnapping of his brother, Sara thought that using his name was far too risky. She would register Simón in her name only. When the official taking the information asked who the father was, Sara shrugged her shoulders and said that the child's father had refused to acknowledge him. The official was sympathetic, telling Sara that men are often foolish about such matters. He had known many such cases, he said, where the father refused to acknowledge the child all through the pregnancy and then melted as soon as he saw the baby. He advised Sara to appeal to his better nature and to all the feelings that had brought about the pregnancy in the first place. There was no hurry, legally they had another week in which to register the child.

Mauricio, by then convinced that it was indeed better if his name didn't surface, was annoyed by the delay. Although the concerned official was disappointed to hear that the father had not changed his mind, he had been right about one thing—Mauricio became a doting father. As soon as Simón cried, he came running. Sent out to buy food, he returned with a toy monkey.

It was a cold winter and Sara was concerned that her baby would get a chill.

"I'll buy a heater," Mauricio said.

"Make it a big kerosene one!"

Sara wrapped herself and Simón in a blanket and curled up on the sofa to feed him. By the time Mauricio returned they were both asleep, and he tiptoed in, carrying a very small heater and a cloth bag. He plugged in the heater and moved it close to the sofa. He gazed at Sara and Simón and thought that he had never seen a lovelier sight. Sara's face was free of worry, her mouth turned up in a slight smile. The brown waves of her hair spread over the pillow made the red of Simón's downy head glimmer in the soft light from the lamp. He reached over to caress her and as he did so, Sara woke. He bent to kiss her, but Sara had already seen the heater.

"Mauricio! An electric heater? Electricity is expensive!"

Determined to preserve the tender feeling that had come over him earlier, Mauricio reached into his shopping bag and pulled out a cloth doll. It was not clear whether it was meant to be male or female, but it had an appealing, smiling face, topped with a mass of red hair. Mauricio pointed at its clothes. "I read somewhere that babies see black and white better than colors. And look—red hair! Like Simón and me!"

For a moment they were a family like any other and Sara laughed in contentment. Simón woke up and Sara and Mauricio made the doll dance for him, wondering if it could possibly be a smile that played over his face as he watched.

Suddenly Sara remembered the call that had come while Mauricio was out. "Your mother telephoned," she said.

Mauricio's happiness vanished. Talking to his mother was a torment.

"What does she want from me?" he said angrily.

"Just that you talk to her."

"And tell her what?" he cried. "That Gerardo is dying and there's nothing I can do to save him?" Pain shot through his left arm like a fire-bolt and he staggered, trying to catch his breath.

Sara put Simón in his basket and ran to the table where Mauricio kept his heart pills. She gave him one and gradually his breathing eased. A doctor, also in hiding, had examined

Mauricio and told him that he was on the brink of a heart attack. He should take it easy. They had all laughed at the suggestion.

She should not have brought up his mother, but Sara felt for the poor woman. Mauricio's silence on the subject of his brother was driving her to despair. All she had been told was that Gerardo had been arrested. His mother wanted to know where he was and whether she could visit him, and Mauricio had not had the heart to tell her the conditions of his imprisonment, only that he was not allowed to receive visitors. Sara had argued that his mother needed to be told the truth, but Mauricio said it would kill her. What was killing her was being kept in the dark, Sara thought, just as what was killing Mauricio was his inability to talk about the guilt and the pain that racked him. None of them talked, she realized. Every so often one of the men would make a reference to a beating he'd been subjected to, but it was always in the context of a joke. The women were a little more open with one another about their fears and worries, but even they kept up a brave front and rarely let down their guard. Perhaps none of them could stop to really consider what was happening to them.

A few days later, when Mauricio said that he was going to another meeting to discuss Gerardo, Sara knew that it was hopeless to argue. These meetings were the only thing that kept his guilt at bay and helped him to believe that he had not given up on his brother and was doing everything he could to save him.

Simón, now three weeks old, was asleep in his wicker basket on the bed next to her, his doll and monkey at his side. Sara was taking in a pair of pants, having already lost most of the weight she'd gained during her pregnancy.

Perhaps the time had come to leave. She and Mauricio had discussed it, but she knew that he would never go while Gerardo was alive. And she? Could she really go until she knew what had happened to Emi, to Jorge, and Mariana? Suddenly, she started, and listened. Was that the sound of cars pulling up outside? She had barely got up from the bed when the front door began to shake. Broken glass showered into the room, followed by fifteen armed men in plain clothes. One of them was Nino Gavazzo. The men scattered to search the kitchen and bathroom. Gavazzo and another man approached Sara.

"Do you remember me?" he asked.

Sara chose not to reply.

"I am Commander Gavazzo of the Uruguayan Armed Forces. And this is Aníbal Gordon. Where is your lover?"

Again Sara did not answer and Gavazzo hit her across the face. She fell back onto the bed and he gave a signal to two of the men who had returned to report that they had found nothing. They took small rubber truncheons out of their pockets and proceeded to hit her on the back and legs. Sara would always remember Simón's basket bouncing up and down on the bed and Simón sleeping soundly through it all as she tried not to cry out and wake him.

The beating over, Sara stood up shakily. The men took pillowcases from the bed and began to fill them with anything they could carry—clothes, cooking utensils, books. What they didn't choose to take, they broke.

"Pick him up," Gordon said, gesturing to Simón.

Sara did, and went to sit with him in a corner, the blood dripping from her nose and mouth onto Simón's blue blanket.

The men searched the basket, tearing the heads off the doll and the monkey, searching inside for papers. One man found a folder hidden among Simón's diapers. He handed it to Gavazzo. "A list of the 'disappeared.'"

"She'll soon be on it," Gavazzo answered. He turned to Sara. "Better leave the baby. You can't take him where you're going."

"He'll be all right, don't worry," Gordon added. "This war isn't against children."

All wars were against children, Sara thought, wishing she'd understood that before she got involved in this one. Believing she was going to her death and would never see him again, she kissed Simón and tucked him into his basket, not taking her eyes off him as her hands were cuffed behind her and a dark plastic bag over her head obliterated him from her sight. As they dragged his mother out to the car, Simón cried for the first time that night.

In the car the plastic bag was replaced with a hood, and they drove off. Before long, Sara sensed the car stopping, and heard the words "Open Sesame!" With a shock, she realized that she was at Automotores Orletti, where Gerardo was, or had been, held.

Sara was aware that Orletti was a torture center established by Aníbal Gordon, nicknamed "the grandfather," due to his reputation for considering children sacred. It was rumored that Gordon would personally kill anyone who even thought of hurting a child. Since children routinely disappeared, and were frequently tortured and terrified by the forces he commanded, it was a mystery how Gordon acquired this reputation.

The car moved forward, stopped, and Sara was taken out. The first sounds she heard as she stepped onto the oil-stained cement floor were the tortured screams coming from the second floor of the building. Sara promised herself that when her time came, she would not utter a sound.

* * *

At the house, the phone was ringing. Mauricio, frantic with worry, had been calling for the last hour, getting no reply. A friend offered to drive him by the house, slowly, as if they were searching for an address. Mauricio immediately saw the broken glass around the front door. He tried to leave the car, but his friend accelerated, refusing to stop until Mauricio threw himself at the steering wheel and brought the car to a halt.

"Let me out! Let me out!" he screamed as his friend threw his arms around him and pinned him down. Mauricio was stronger and more desperate and would have won in the end if he had not collapsed against the seat, barely able to breathe.

* * *

It was customary to greet prisoners with a beating, and that night was no exception.

The beatings over, files were opened for each of the eighteen men and women taken that night, all Uruguayan. They were asked their names and date of birth. The date of their detention was also included in the file, and in an effort not only to eliminate personal identity but also to ensure that names didn't leak out, a number was assigned to each one and hung around the prisoner's neck. From now on, this number, not their names, would be used to summon them for torture in the so-called "operating theatres," on rare visits to the toilet, and for "transference"—a euphemism for assassination.

Sara had heard of children being used to obtain confessions from their parents, and it was her greatest fear. Perhaps the men assigned to extract information from her didn't know about her son Simón, and if she could stop herself from asking them what had become of him, his existence might remain a secret. She knew that the best protection for Simón would be never to mention him. But how to prevent her mind from dwelling on him, from wondering what had happened to him, from tormenting herself with thoughts that he might be hungry, or cold, or abandoned somewhere to die?

It was icy cold on the oily cement floor of the old garage where Sara lay with several other prisoners. All of them were hooded, their feet chained or tied, and their hands manacled behind them.

Under the constant din of the radio that played day and night to cover the screams of those being tortured, they managed to engage in whispered conversations, huddling together in a fruitless effort to keep warm.

* * *

When her turn came to go up the cement stairway to the "operating theatre"—in this case the two rooms known as the confession chamber and the truth chamber, Sara was surprised by the mixture of anticipation and anxiety she felt. She had been preparing for this extreme experience ever since she first learned what went on behind the walls of places like Orletti. Everyone involved in the guerrilla movements asked themselves how they would respond when the time came to enter a torture chamber. Some refused to think about it, others dwelled on torture and tried to plan ahead. It was not unusual for guerrillas to carry cyanide tablets along with a piece of glass, which they would crunch with the poison, cutting their mouths to accelerate the rate of absorption. Sara had prepared by envisioning and attempting to recreate the methods of torture, forcing herself to think in detail about her physical and mental reaction to extreme pain. She was anxious to test herself, and climbed the stairs leading to the torture chambers faster than she was being driven, causing the soldier guarding her to remark, "Look at this madwoman, she's smiling!"

In the truth chamber, her hands were cuffed behind her and wires coiled around her waist. Sara was hung from her wrists from a hook in the ceiling until her feet were several inches off the floor. The pain was excruciating. Sara discovered the only benefit of the hood—it would conceal her efforts to keep herself quiet.

"We'll see you in about an hour!" the men said. "Behave yourself!"

* * *

By the time the men returned, the pain was so pervasive Sara did not know where it began and her body ended, she was just a hurting mass of twisted muscles, and she could feel the blood running down her arms where the handcuffs had chafed her skin raw. Although she knew that the worst was yet to come, it was almost a relief to hear the men's voices as they entered the room.

"Are you ready for us?"

Sara felt something being placed around her hips. "There's a wand on this belt, and we'll be tickling you with it. It's attached to a cable plugged into the wall."

While the device was being set up, the Argentines in the room boasted of their invention, while the Uruguayans bragged about their very particular skill at using it. Sara heard the sounds of water being spilled on the floor, and one of the men told her that they would also be sprinkling it with salt. She would be lowered until her toes touched it. "You'll try to lift your feet when we turn the current on," he said, "but you've been hanging for a long time and you won't be able to."

Every cell in her body seemed to explode when the current was turned on. She could no longer move her head, and the numbness in her arms and legs made her wonder if the shocks had paralyzed her. Something in the place where her legs were tried to lift her feet, which felt on fire, but the message never reached its destination, and the floor burned on in what Sara later described as an "orgy of pain."

She came to as she heard men returning. One of them attempted to lower her. Her body was so charged with electricity that he received a shock for his efforts, shouting at his companions to turn off the current. They laughed. It had been off for quite a while.

"What's that?" he asked, pointing to the floor.

There was a moment of silence and a different voice said, "Milk."

Sara had not noticed that her breasts had been leaking while she was suspended above the floor.

The pain of being un-hung was different to anything she'd experienced so far. For a moment it felt as if her arms had been detached from her body and everything inside her was tipped upside down. She could not see her hands, but she heard one of the soldiers comment on their pretty purple color.

Back on the downstairs floor, Sara understood why people begged for water after electric shock torture. The shocks caused dehydration and the desire for water was overwhelming. Even if it had been available, her fellow prisoner Margarita told her, it would have been dangerous to drink, so she should try to focus on something else. Immediately, Sara thought of Simón, and again brought all her strength to bear on obliterating any memory of him.

Over the next few days, Sara became all too familiar with the screeching of the metal door, and the password "Open Sesame" that could he heard over the interphone before the door opened. On the floor, every position accompanied by a stab of pain, or by involuntary contact, causing pain to another, their voices whispered, "Resist, companions, this is where revolutionaries graduate!"

Resisting, not giving information, not confessing, keeping one another strong, and providing what comfort was possible when they were all injured from the beatings and torture, starved, humiliated, and unable to perform the most basic rites of personal cleanliness, was the code by which they lived and bore the passage of interminable days.

* * *

"I'm falling! I'm falling!"

Sara and Margarita were lying back-to-back. Sara grabbed Margarita's hand. "You're on the floor, you can't fall! Hold on!

You won't fall as long as you hold on!"

"Which way up am I?"

"Your feet are toward the door," Sara said, with no idea if this was true.

Margarita's breathing gradually quieted and she relaxed her hold on Sara's hand.

Hooding brought about a loss of spatial awareness, a heightened tension, since one could be attacked at any moment without warning. None of them knew what was coming, or what their surroundings were like. Some of them imagined the area in which they were being held as round; others thought of it as a kind of football stadium, with the guards circling over their heads.

Sara had also learned that the sensation that her feet had been on fire was real. During electric torture, the soles of the feet were burnt and layers of hard skin formed, peeling off later. The application of electricity also provoked vomiting and uncontrolled defecation. It would have been inconceivable before this to imagine how sharing such conditions would bring human beings closer together, but in the blindness of the hood, in the absence of comfort of any kind, everything except supporting one another became irrelevant.

At times, their own smell was unbearable, and they would gag and retch, their empty stomachs in knots. Occasionally, one of them felt that he was dying, and the others would roll toward him, rallying him to give the bastards another run for their money. That was the only way to get through it. If one imagined that the torture, the filth and the cold would last forever, one went mad.

They shared one thin mattress, soon impregnated with urine, vomit, sweat and blood. Sleep was hard to come by, disruptions constant, following no predictable routine, and hygiene was virtually non-existent.

They knew that many of the men who came and went from Orletti, transporting and questioning prisoners, were their countrymen. It was no surprise that the armed forces of Argentina and Uruguay were collaborating in their attempt to wipe out the guerrillas. What the prisoners couldn't understand was the viciousness of their methods.

In the event that bodies were needed for mock gun battles with police or armed services personnel, prisoners were washed and fed for a few days. In some cases they were given injections to make them sleepy before they were killed. They would then appear in the news as "extremists killed in shoot-outs."

How had things got so out of control? they asked each other. How had they gone from being a band of brothers to being fugitives labeled as terrorists? Had they been fools to talk of "the masses," delegating everyone but themselves into an amorphous group of people unable or unwilling to take charge of their own destiny? Had they been naïve to believe that people would immediately understand what was at stake and would therefore side with them against the government and the military?

Sara remembered how deeply Mauricio resented thinking that he had been manipulated, taken for a fool. Things had gone wrong, yes, but not for the reasons their enemies gave. They were not power hungry, but they genuinely believed that the country would be better off in different hands. How had they failed to anticipate the degree of the violence that would be unleashed against them?

These questions ran through Sara's head as she attempted to keep track of time and of the passage of days by the radio. She estimated that she had been at Orletti for five days, each one a carbon copy of the one before—beatings, torture, increasing thirst and hunger, infections running rampant, smells no longer noticeable. Then one night there was a party to celebrate the shooting of a subversive. Sara could hear corks popping, and as the night progressed the men got drunker and drunker, until one of them suggested including the prisoners in the party.

Not knowing what that might mean, they all tensed as they heard the men coming toward them. Hands groped their heads and pulled off their hoods. As their eyes adjusted to the dim light, they tried to get their bearings, but it was difficult to see beyond the men surrounding them, offering them drinks of champagne. They were parched with thirst, and would have preferred water. That, however, was not an option. When Sara asked for it, the man offering her the champagne simply said, "Go thirsty, then!" and was about to stagger away when Sara said she would take it. He held the bottle to her lips and she took a long drink. Almost immediately, dizziness overcame her and she would have fallen if she had been upright. The remains of the meat, bread, and pizza were offered to them next and they ate greedily, regretting it at once. Several of them bent over with cramps, one or two vomited.

The men capped off their evening by approaching one of the prisoners, a young man named Carlos, whose leg wounds had turned gangrenous. They offered to take him to a doctor, and Carlos, who was delirious, agreed to accompany them. They dragged him up the stairs. The prisoners left behind heard the sounds of sloshing water. A few minutes later, the men returned.

"Carlos is fine," they said. "We sent him to Doctor Saint Peter!"

* * *

While Carlos was being drowned at Orletti, a few select guests, among them the United States ambassador, gathered at the home of a wealthy businessman in the Montevideo suburb of Carrasco. The meeting had been arranged for the benefit of the commanders-in-chief of the Navy, Army, and Air Force, and the head of the joint military and police forces.

Legislation had recently been approved in the United States requiring that the Secretary of State prepare human rights reports at Congress' request, and demanding that countries receiving weapons from the US not engage in internationally recognized human rights violations. The report prepared by the State Department regarding Argentina had been unequivocal in its condemnation of the terrorism being practiced by the left and the right wing forces, and in its recognition that the right wing terrorists were acting under the auspices of the government. It had erred in its estimate of the use of torture, which it had deemed to be rare. Democrat Edward Koch, State Representative for New York, was determined to suspend military aid to all the Latin American dictatorships, including a cut of five million dollars a year for Uruguay, which Koch had characterized as "Latin America's Torture Chamber." Uruguay held the dubious distinction of having the highest ratio of political prisoners in proportion to its population, outdoing even Argentina and Chile. Koch's opponents argued that the military of South America were waging war against international Communism, and that their countries would fall into the hands of terrorists without American military aid.

Uruguay had been planning to request seven-and-a-half-million dollars for 1977, and the commanders meeting with the ambassador wanted to know how they could prevent Representative Koch from succeeding with his congressional proposal.

"Koch," the ambassador said, "has very high principles. I have no idea how he ever got into politics."

The businessman hosting the gathering, laughed politely. The others, now very much involved in politics themselves, weren't at all sure if this was funny.

"Why would he concern himself over a few measly millions of dollars?" the brigadier inquired.

"If it was that measly, we wouldn't be concerning ourselves either, would we, gentlemen?" the ambassador said.

The others humored the ambassador with a laugh, joined this time by the general, who thought it a good dig at the brigadier.

"I don't find it in the least amusing to have my country described in the international press as 'Latin America's torture chamber,'" the admiral said sternly.

"Koch was confusing us with Argentina," the general added.

"You have been far too successful, gentlemen," the ambassador replied. "You've wiped out a guerrilla movement. I foresee decades of consulting work before you. Clearly, you are under no internal security threat and need no additional funding from us."

The four commanders exchanged looks.

"We have a proposal," the general said.

"I'm listening."

"You've intimated that if we can prove that the subversives are planning to blow up businesses—like our good host's here, which enjoys the benefit of capital from many fine American enterprises—"

"Yes, yes," the ambassador replied impatiently, anxious to leave this meeting.

". . . and that they intend to kidnap and assassinate leading financial and political figures, then perhaps your Congress can be swayed."

The ambassador gave a small, difficult to interpret, nod.

"We are holding thirty of these subversives in Buenos Aires, in—"

"No details."

"We'll let it be known that they're planning to come back," the admiral put in. "We'll bomb a few places, not hurting anybody, of course."

"The less I know the better, gentlemen," the ambassador reminded them.

"You get the idea."

"I can imagine that if these ruthless guerrillas did venture to leave Buenos Aires and come here, you would spare no effort to capture them. Confessions would be extracted. There would be a press conference."

"Whatever you say," the brigadier agreed.

"I am not issuing instructions," the ambassador snapped. "Just speculating."

"I will persuade my American business partners that the threat is real," their host said, speaking for the first time. "And—"

"It is real!" said the admiral.

"And plead with them to use their influence with their senators and representatives."

"And I," said the ambassador, "will of course need to notify the State Department—where we have some very good friends in high places—that you have alerted us to this terrorist threat."

The next day, Nino Gavazzo received instructions to proceed to Buenos Aires to repatriate twenty-four Uruguayans. His orders were not well received at Orletti, where prisoners rarely left alive to tell the tale. Gavazzo explained that they were needed to stage an invasion. His Argentine colleagues wanted to know whether the confessions couldn't be obtained first and the invaders killed on arrival in Uruguay? Gavazzo did not see how he could possibly make that credible. If not confessions, then couldn't their plans be "discovered," so to speak, after they were killed? Gavazzo reminded his colleagues that the Condor Plan agreement stated very clearly that the final determination of a prisoner's fate lay with their country of origin, successfully persuading them to allow him to take twenty-four of his countrymen and women.

* * *

Sara and the other prisoners selected for this operation knew nothing of these machinations, and when their handcuffs and hoods were removed, they were left staring at each another. Their first thought was to wonder if they themselves looked as wretched as the others. Some were naked, others wore the remains of various items of clothing. Their hair was matted with blood, and the burns all over their bodies covered in filth. A few had eye infections and could barely see, and all were shaky on their feet. All they could think was that their time had come to die, but then they were allowed to sip some *mate*. Holding the gourd was difficult for most of them. Their hands were swollen, and a few had lost all feeling in their arms.

They were in a deplorable state, and any shame they might have felt at standing before one another smelling of blood, vomit, and excrement, disappeared in mutual compassion. They were permitted to wash, and to choose items of clothing from a pile in a corner. Once they were dressed, they were given some bread and more *mate*. It was not uncommon for those who were going to be killed in mock shootouts with the police to be washed and fed first, and believing that this was to be their fate, some of them cried as they said goodbye to one another.

Their mouths were taped shut and the hoods put on again. Their hands were handcuffed, and they were loaded into various cars. After a time, they heard the sound of airplanes, and Sara's conviction that they were going to die increased. She knew of the practice of dumping bodies, dead and alive, into the Río de la Plata. She thought of her mother and father, of her sisters, of Mauricio, and finally allowed herself to dwell on thoughts of Simón.

The car stopped and Sara was led up steps and into an airplane. She expected to be thrown to the floor but was instead seated and a seat belt placed around her. Surely, they wouldn't have bothered with safety measures if she was going to be thrown off the plane.

Not long after takeoff, the plane landed again, and Sara sat up straighter, all her senses on the alert.

She and her companions were helped down to the tarmac and told to walk up a ramp. Many of them had difficulty doing so.

The ramp was steep, and the emotions of the last few hours had drained them of the little strength they had. A new voice, one they hadn't heard before, reassured them. "Hang on! We know you're in bad shape. It's a short trip and as soon as you get there you'll be better, you'll see!" Hands supported them as they climbed the ramp, and guided them onto hard wooden benches.

About twenty minutes later, the truck stopped, the engine was turned off, and in the silence that followed they heard the welcome and familiar sound of gulls. Was it possible that they were back in Montevideo?

Leaving the truck, they climbed some steps and heard a door open and close behind them. Their hoods and the tape sealing their mouths were removed, and they found themselves in a house, almost bare of furniture, and with all the blinds drawn so they could not see out. The soldiers guarding them wore Uruguayan military uniforms.

Their handcuffs were removed and they were taken into the dining room. The keys to Sara's cuffs could not be found, and a soldier was dispatched to look for them while the prisoners sat at the table, on chairs by the wall, or on the floor. Soon, two soldiers came in, bearing large trays with bowls of custard, sweet, warm and easy to swallow and digest.

When they had finished, they were told that they would be allowed to shower and that clean clothes were waiting for them upstairs. Sara was the last to go up the stairs to the bathroom, the keys to her cuffs finally located. The young soldier on duty in the bathroom turned his back partially toward Sara as she began to undress, but her right arm was paralyzed and she could not use her fingers.

"Please ask one of the other women to come up and help me."

"I can't," the soldier said, "it's against regulations."

Again Sara tried to undress and again she failed.

"I'll help you if you want me to," the soldier said.

Sara had been naked so often during the last few weeks her body so abused that she could not imagine anything this young man could do that would alter the feeling that her body was an object separate from herself. Perhaps all he wanted was a good look, perhaps he'd steal a grope or try a clumsy caress. She didn't care. She was going to have a hot shower and there was a lot she'd suffer gladly for that privilege, so she nodded, and the soldier leaned his gun against the wall.

Sara was totally unprepared for the tenderness and respect with which he proceeded to remove her clothes, careful not to hurt her further. He eased her shirt over her cut wrists and hands, and knelt to untie her shoes. She sat on the toilet seat and he made sure the laces were loose before he took the shoes off. He opened the cuffs of the socks wide, so the wool didn't scrape the burns on her feet. He undid the buttons on her trousers and again, eased her out of them. As the wounds on her legs, her belly and her breasts were fully revealed the tears he had been holding back began trickling down his cheeks. He draped her shirt over her shoulders tenderly, sat her back on the toilet seat and found towels to wrap her in. "A bath will be better for you," he said. "The shower might hurt."

He ran the water until it was just the right temperature and filled the tub. He helped Sara in, and with the same care with which he had removed her clothes, soaked a sponge and squeezed the water gently over her arms and back. "There ... there," he said, "that must feel good."

Sara had not felt so cared for since she was a child.

That night she slept on a clean mattress, one of two rows of mattresses arranged in an orderly fashion along the walls of two large bedrooms. In sharp contrast to the chaos and fetid smells of Orletti, everything smelled clean, and for the first time in almost two weeks, Sara slept without hearing screams.

When she woke it was still dark outside. The room was lit by a small night light near the door and the only sound was a faint snore from one of her companions. She was warm, she was clothed, and there was a glass of water by her bed. Her arm hurt as she reached for it. In fact, when she stopped to think about it, her entire body hurt, but somehow it didn't matter. She could think of her baby Simón now, she could remember how the winter sun had made his red hair gleam, how it had felt to bathe him for the first time, his skin so smooth and slippery she had been afraid she would drop him, and how he had kept falling asleep at her breast, the milk trickling down his cheek toward his ear.

It had been many years since she'd prayed, and she wasn't sure who she was praying to, since the God of her childhood had taken on the quality of myth. But pray she did, to whatever benign force might exist. She gave thanks for another day of life, for being out of Orletti, and prayed that Simón was alive and cared for, and that one day she would hold him again, ask for his forgiveness, tell him why she had wanted him so desperately, how he had represented hope, an investment in a better future.

She fell asleep again, and when she woke the next day, she was taken to breakfast and then examined by a doctor, who prescribed iron supplements and ordered complete bed rest.

Later that day, the same soldier who had bathed her brought her a tray of food. Mashed potatoes and pumpkin, and stewed prunes.

"Why are we being treated so well?" Sara asked him.

"We have much more scientific torture techniques than the Argentines," he smiled sadly. "Here you confess or go crazy."

* * *

The general was on the telephone. He was incensed, and his tone barely polite. He was holding several sheets of paper and waving them impatiently in the air. "Do you know what I am holding in my hand?" he said, his voice quivering with rage.

Hearing the United States ambassador's response, the general bristled. "There's no need to be crude, Mr. Ambassador," he said. "What I am holding is an excerpt from your Congressional Record! Your State Department informed Congress that Uruguay's internal security was threatened by a terrorist commando unit which we've neutralized . . . What's wrong with that? The terrorist commando unit is sitting in a safe house! Where we put them. Our press knows nothing of the threat yet. We'll look like fools!"

Later that day, while fencing with the admiral, the general was still irate. "And do you know what that American bastard said to me?" He advanced aggressively on his companion who parried and backed away. "'Who will pay any attention to what's happening in Uruguay? Let alone notice any discrepancy in the dates.'"

"He's right," the Admiral said. "We'll just go ahead as planned, although I'm liking this less and less."

"Has Gavazzo got his confessions yet?"

"They're refusing to sign."

"Like hell they are!" the general said, scoring a hit. "Tell him to tighten the screws."

The Admiral had medals for fencing, but today the general was beating him soundly. "This is not Argentina," he said, backing up.

"I'll say not. Daily showers, bed linen, three meals a day, a doctor on duty twenty-four hours."

"We can't present them to the press looking like they just came out of Auschwitz!"

"Tell Gavazzo to offer them whatever they want!"

"But—"

"For God's sake! As if any of it will be binding."

* * *

The prisoners were summoned to a meeting, and to their surprise, their hoods were removed. They soon realized why.

"You already know me," Gavazzo said. "And you owe your lives to the humanitarianism of our Armed Forces." He walked around the room, studying them. "Does anyone want to return to Buenos Aires?"

No one answered and Gavazzo laughed. "I want you to remember that no one knows where you are. Officially, you don't exist. Your lives will be spared, if you sign a confession saying that you were captured here. Refuse and you'll go back to Argentina. Agree, and you'll spend a couple of years behind bars. Those who don't want to cooperate remain standing; the others may sit."

They all sat.

"Very good. I'll have the papers drawn up."

Once they were back in their quarters, they agreed that if they were still alive it was because something was required of them, they were of use somehow, otherwise the whole process of saving them and bringing them to Montevideo, feeding them and tending to their ills, made no sense.

"We'll negotiate," Margarita said.

They began by refusing to sign the confessions Gavazzo put before them, including statements that they were part of a larger plot that included murder, sabotage, and the placement of explosives. He had them beaten and tried again a few days later. He had no better luck with them this time.

* * *

While Gavazzo was attempting to stage the invasion of his country by terrorists, the wheels of the Condor Plan were turning within the United States.

After a meeting in 1976 between Henry Kissinger and Chilean General Augusto Pinochet, Kissinger let the dictator know that in the United States the general was sympathetically regarded for his efforts to wipe out communism. Encouraged by such praise, the general expressed his concern over the presence in Washington D.C. of Dr. Orlando Letelier, former Chilean ambassador for the Allende government, and a leader of Chile's Socialist Party. Letelier had also previously worked at the Bank for International Development. He was at home in Washington, where he chose to live after international pressure had forced Pinochet to release him after a year of imprisonment.

In March, Letelier had appeared before a congressional committee. His revelations led not only to the suspension of military aid to Chile, but to a congressional investigation into the role of the CIA in the overthrow of President Salvador Allende.

Pinochet was incensed that Letelier's influence wasn't limited to the US, where good friends like Henry Kissinger would control the damage. Several non-aligned countries had broken off diplomatic relations with Chile after President Allende's murder and the overthrow of his government, and Letelier was blamed for the ruptures. In Holland, striking dock-workers refused to load goods for the Chilean *Junta,* and Pinochet saw Letelier's influence behind that protest as well. Untiring in his efforts to bring to light events in Latin America, Letelier was coauthoring a book with his friend Michael Moffit about the new international economic order.

On the evening of September 20, Michael Moffit and his wife Ronni dined with Letelier at his home in Washington D.C. Letelier had just heard that as a result of his activities, Pinochet's regime was depriving him of Chilean citizenship.

"I got lucky!" he joked. "There were some who voted to have me assassinated instead!"

"September always makes me nervous," Letelier's wife Isabel said.

"Killing month in Chile," Letelier agreed.

September 11, 1973, had marked the overthrow of Allende's government and the slaughter that followed. In the two Septembers since, General Carlos Prats González—Commander-in-Chief of the Chilean Army under President Allende—and his wife Sofía had been assassinated in Buenos Aires. An attempt was also made on the lives of Bernardo Leighton, a critic of the Chilean military, and his wife, Anita.

"It just wasn't my turn. I've gained another year!"

But September wasn't over yet.

Michael and Ronni Moffit borrowed the Letelier's car for their drive home to Maryland and were back in D.C. early the next morning to pick up Letelier. Isabel reminded her husband that she was meeting him downtown for lunch.

Letelier drove, with Ronni in the passenger seat next to him and her husband Michael in the back. They turned onto Embassy Row and were deep in a discussion, when there was a flash of light, a high-pitched whistle, and a ball of fire consumed the car.

Two Israeli diplomats traveling in the car behind skidded past the explosion and were showered with glass and metal. Believing themselves the target of the attack, they left their car and huddled together in a cloud of black smoke, trying to assess the damage to themselves and their vehicle.

Outside the Turkish embassy, a policeman lay prostrate and semiconscious, on the ground next to him was an attaché from the Greek embassy, temporarily blinded. The remains of Letelier's car had crashed into a parked Volkswagen that jumped the curb and came straight at the Greek attaché. He was saved by a No Parking sign that stopped the Volkswagen about a foot from his body. Fearing more explosions, the attaché groped his way to the nearest building. As his eyesight cleared, he saw that it was the Irish Embassy, and thinking that the attack might have been the work of Irish terrorists, he ran the other way, only to find himself back at the Turkish embassy, where he surmised that a Greek such as himself would be not only unwelcome, but highly suspect. Again he ran, this time toward his own embassy across Massachusetts Avenue.

By now, two guards who were part of an Executive Protection Service had arrived on the scene. The smell of gunpowder and burned flesh reached them before they got out of their car. There was glass everywhere, and amid the debris they saw a shoe with a foot still in it. They were trying to open the driver's door in what remained of the exploded car when they saw a spark and jumped back, running to get a fire extinguisher from their vehicle.

Michael Moffit had managed to extricate himself from the burning wreckage and tried desperately to open the driver's door. His hair was burned, his face blackened, and his shirt torn. "Assassins! Fascists!" he cried, desperately trying to pull Orlando Letelier's body from the car. Ronni Moffit, meanwhile had dragged herself out of the passenger window and was lying on the grass by the curb. Blood dripped from beneath the door.

A young anesthetist who had heard the explosion from her car several blocks away rushed to the scene. She ran to Ronni's side, saw that she was choking, and pushed her head back, scooping blood clots from her mouth with her fingers and telling Ronni to breathe. Ronni tried, but it was a losing battle, she was drowning in her own blood. Suddenly the anesthetist felt herself being grasped and shaken from behind.

"Save her!" Michael Moffit shouted. "Save her!"

She tried to calm him and turned back to Ronni, who was fading fast, and began CPR, pausing every so often to remove the blood pooling in the oxygen mask one of the policemen had brought.

By the time they heard the ambulances arriving on the scene, it was too late.

* * *

Twenty minutes after the blast, Isabel Letelier received a telephone call notifying her that her husband had been in a car accident. She took a cab to the hospital and found it full of people. Michael Moffit came sobbing toward her, repeating the word "bomb" over and over. FBI agents took her aside and told her what had happened. Isabel asked to see her husband's body.

"Spare yourself, Mrs. Letelier," the agents said, "it would be best to remember him as he was when he left home this morning."

"I want to see my husband's body," Isabel repeated. "Even if all that remains of it is a hand, I will bid it farewell."

* * *

In accordance with the pattern used so far to explain Condor Plan assassinations to the public, CIA Director George H. W. Bush reported that the murders were "a settling of accounts between leftists." This time, however, Ronni Moffit, a US citizen, had been killed, and neither the press, nor Michael Moffit, nor Orlando Letelier's family, were buying the story. They demanded an investigation. The reply from the Justice Department inquired if what they wanted was another Watergate.

More than a decade later, on December 22, 1992, former chief of Chilean intelligence, General Manuel Contreras, accused the CIA—in whose pay he had once been—of having ordered the 1974 murder of Carlos Prats and his wife in Buenos Aires, and of hiring former CIA Agent Michael Townley to do the job.*

---

* Seventeen years after the attack on the Leightons in Rome, Townley received a fifteen year sentence for his participation in the failed assassination.

General Contreras' revelations did not stop there. He accused former president George H.W. Bush of being a knowledgeable party to all these actions, and refused to offer himself up as the sacrificial goat for crimes he said were planned in Washington. General Contreras served a seven-year sentence for his part in the murder of Orlando Letelier and Ronni Moffit, and in February of 2003, in an ongoing effort to bring the Condor Plan conspirators to justice, he was indicted in Chile for the murder of General Carlos Prats and his wife Sofía Cuthbert.

* * *

It was October before an agreement was reached with the prisoners in Montevideo. Sara and her companions consented to cooperate in mounting an invasion, in exchange for being publicly recognized as prisoners, the only way they could see of safeguarding their lives. The most powerful card Gavazzo held was his threat to return them to Buenos Aires, where they would disappear, in all likelihood forever.

There were to be two phases to his plan. Phase I entailed selecting sixteen prisoners and assigning a member of army intelligence to each of them. The prisoners quickly realized that the men and women assigned to them resembled them closely. They were of the same gender, height, build, and coloring. A few days before Phase II went into effect, their doubles left the house and the prisoners did not see them again.

As part of Phase II, on a Saturday morning in late October, Sara and four companions were loaded into two cars by half a dozen men in casual civilian clothing and driven out of the city along the coastal highway. They stopped at a roadside stall and Margarita and one of the men left the car to buy vegetables. While her companion was busy paying for their purchase, Margarita caught the stall keeper's eye and casually rolled up her sleeves. Her arms and wrists were healing, but the evidence of her sores and burns was enough to make the stall keeper's eyes widen momentarily. Margarita would be remembered.

Their next stop was at a butcher's, and this time Sara and her male companion went inside to buy ribs and sausages. When her partner handed her the meat, Sara feigned clumsiness, and managed to grasp his coat along with the package, revealing his holster and gun. Like the vegetable seller, the butcher would remember this sale.

They drove on through one or two seaside resorts, mostly closed for the season, and finally pulled up outside a small chalet. A sign in the garden identified it as the Chalet Susy. They were taken into the house and out into the back garden, where the outside grill was fired up and the meat set to roasting.

It was the first time in months that Sara had been outside and she could not believe how good it felt. It was cool and sunny. Sara lay face down on the grass to feel her heart beating against the earth. Margarita sat next to her, lifting her face to the sun.

"What do you think they're up to?" she asked Sara softly.

"At this moment I don't care!"

As soon as the meat was cooked, the men cut up the bread they had brought and opened a bottle of wine. Other guests would be joining them, they said. At four o'clock, the prisoners were to go inside and wait. If they attempted to escape, they would be shot. The troops that would be descending on the house had been ordered to capture the terrorists living there and had not been informed about the details of this secret operation.

Sara and the others focused on enjoying the outdoors and the food. The meat and sausages were tasty and well cooked, and the bread crusty and fresh. All of them, prisoners and guards, drank little. It was almost five before an order came over the radio carried by a Captain Medina, instructing them to go inside. Sara and the others were taken into a bedroom with iron bars on the windows and told not to move until someone came for them.

Margarita opened the closet doors. "Look," she said to the others, holding up some papers.

Sara felt faint. The papers Margarita had found were those she and Mauricio had moved from their house to the Juliens when Gerardo was arrested. "The Juliens," she murmured. "They must have fallen too. They had two children . . ." The painful thought that little Anatole and Eva had probably disappeared along with Simón, brought back all the old feelings of helplessness and panic. Perhaps all three children were dead, or in an orphanage, or had fallen into the hands of people who would abuse them for their parents' actions.

* * *

Roger Julien and his wife Victoria Grisonas disappeared on September 26, 1976. Major Gavazzo and his team broke into their house through a back alley. Roger Julien hid his two children in the bathtub and went out the front door to surrender. Once out on the pavement, he was shot, along with his wife, who was repeatedly thrown up in the air and allowed to fall to the ground until she lost consciousness. Their two children, four-year-old Anatole and one-year-old Eva, saw their father's dead body and their mother lying unconscious on the pavement outside their house as they were put into a car and taken to Orletti. In mid-October, they were found wandering in a plaza in Chile where they had been abandoned. They were put up for adoption and remained with their adoptive family after their grandmother found them three years later. When they were older they were made aware of their history.

* * *

There could be only two reasons why materials belonging to the Juliens were in the house—to prove to them that these friends too had been taken, and to serve as evidence against them in court. How stupid she had been, Sara thought, to allow herself to imagine that by leaving hints of their identity at the markets on their way to the Chalet Suzy they might be rescued. So long as her son Simón and others like him were missing, Gavazzo and his kind would have the upper hand.

The quiet of the afternoon was shattered by the shrill scream of sirens. The few neighbors who lived year-long at the seaside resort of Shangri-La had witnessed the unloading of boxes earlier that month by people clearly behaving in a secretive and evasive manner as they carried their cargo into the chalet. Now they were treated to the sight of a convoy of jeeps blazing with lights and full of armed soldiers. A megaphone was used to order the occupants of the chalet to exit with their hands over their heads. When no one appeared, several soldiers jumped from the jeeps. They ran toward the house, threw themselves to the ground, rolled toward the garden walls, and vaulted over them. The neighbors, who had never seen anything like this except at the movies, watched in wonder from behind the safety of their curtains as the man who appeared to be in charge kicked in the door of the Chalet Susy and entered, accompanied by a handful of soldiers. The neighbors marveled at his courage and expected any moment to hear gunfire and see the brave commander's body flung back out the door.

Inside the chalet, Sara heard laughter. The door to their room opened and, amid much joking, she, her four companions, and three of the military intelligence men impersonating the "subversives" were handcuffed and blindfolded.

With heightened interest and admiration for the commander and his men, the neighbors watched while the "terrorists" were marched out, along with "the extensive cache of arms they had smuggled into the chalet."

The seven of them were loaded into the jeeps and the convoy drove away, lights and sirens blaring. Several cars and military trucks joined the procession as it advanced toward the city. Captain Medina, who was one of those pretending to be a captive, got very excited and lifted his blindfold so he could look out. A sharp order came over the radio for him to stop "fucking about."

The operation had been carefully timed to coincide with the exit from the stadium of a large crowd who had been attending a match between Peñarol and Nacional, the country's two most popular soccer teams. The departing fans were treated to a lengthy display of their armed forces driving slowly by in the crush of traffic bearing away the latest threat to the nation's security.

Later that evening, the Phase I intelligence personnel look-alikes who had been assigned days before to study the prisoners, were also "arrested." They had been in Buenos Aires and returned to Uruguay using false documentation in the name of the prisoner they had been assigned to impersonate. They had checked into various hotels and were now taken into custody.

Uruguayans were informed that, thanks to the alert response of special units of the armed forces, sixty-two terrorists had been taken, including five of their leaders, one of whom was Sara Méndez.

Until that moment, Sara's family knew only that she had disappeared from Buenos Aires, and her father had been searching the morgues and hospitals in Argentina for her.

The communiqué issued to the press listed only seventeen of the sixty-two, but sixty-two was the number of missing Uruguayans reported by their exiled countrymen and by human rights organizations monitoring events from outside the country. Stating that sixty-two had been arrested made it appear that all of them were accounted for. All three dailies picked up the story and photos were printed of the firearms that had been found in a hollow under the fireplace of the Chalet Susy.

Back at the safe house, Sara and her companions were ordered to spend time outdoors, sunbathing in the rather weak spring sunshine. They were due to be presented to the press in a few days' time and since they were supposed to have been at liberty plotting the "invasion" every effort was being made to alleviate the deathly pallor caused by months of imprisonment.

When the time came to present them to the press, they were taken back to the Chalet Susy, which they barely recognized. It was riddled with bullets and every piece of furniture damaged. The group due to be presented to the press was ushered into the same room in which Sara had found evidence of the Julien's arrest the week before. From there they could hear Major Gavazzo, who was in charge of the press conference, apologizing for the condition of the house, caused, he explained, by the struggle to apprehend the terrorists. The journalists were mainly interested in seeing the terrorists themselves, but Gavazzo was not to be hurried.

"This most recent, but by no means last attempt," he said, "to reactivate terror in Uruguay, was planned by the *Movimiento de Liberación Nacional Tupamaro* refugees in Argentina, where in the shelter provided by our sister nation, they continued the crimes they had begun here. They transferred a cell to Uruguay after carrying out self-kidnappings in Buenos Aires, which were reported to the Argentine authorities as 'disappearances.'"

"This," he said, gesturing to the sad remains of the chalet, "was the principal center of operations for this band. And here," he said, moving to a table on which was displayed a veritable arsenal of weapons, "are the arms the terrorists were trained to use in Cuba and Argentina. You will soon," he said, "enjoy an opportunity of seeing these so-called guerrillas for yourselves, but let me remind you that only a judge will be allowed to question them."

With much fanfare, Sara and the others were filed before the flashing cameras. A few daring journalists called out questions, but the only reply they received was a burst of laughter from Sara and Margarita.

Unaware of the painstaking drama being staged on their behalf, the United States Congress voted against the renewal of military aid to Uruguay.

* * *

In accordance with the laws passed at the time of the military takeover, Margarita and Sara were to be tried by a military tribunal. They were given a choice between military or civilian defense lawyers. They chose civilian ones. When Major Gavazzo learned of it, he arranged for the civilian lawyers to resign, and assigned the prisoners military attorneys. Sara's was a Colonel Rodríguez, who she did not see once during the entire proceedings, and who never responded to her requests for a meeting.

Both Margarita and Sara were sentenced to four-and-a-half years in what the military dubbed "the ladies boarding school." It was an old convent, converted by the military into a women's prison. It housed two hundred prisoners divided into four sectors—red, yellow, blue, and black. The red sector was considered the most dangerous, and it was here that both Sara and Margarita were placed in a large room with eight other women. The windows had bars, and the glass had been painted white so the women could not see out. The floors were parquet, kept well shined by the inmates.

Sara was issued the regulation gray pants and top, with a red breast pocket and the number 349 printed on the back. She spent her first night in prison listening to the cries of a newborn baby, whose mother had just returned from the military hospital where she had given birth. Sara kept imagining that it was Simón, calling to her for help.

A Captain Martínez was assigned to go to Sara's family home to pick up underclothes, nightwear, and toiletries for her, and Sara asked him to inquire after Simón. The Captain did so, and he seemed both surprised and worried when he reported back to Sara that Simón was not with them and that her family knew nothing of his whereabouts.

"He was probably there," he said reassuringly, "but you know how it is. If he was given to them secretly, brought in illegally, they would never admit it to me."

Sara knew that this was a reasonable assumption, but if they really didn't know where he was, what then had happened to Mauricio? Had he been taken at the same time she had? Or had he managed to go into hiding with Simón? It would be three weeks before she was allowed a family visit and could begin to piece together what had happened to Mauricio and their son.

Meanwhile, Sara was thankful for the routine of prison life. The day at Punta de Rieles began at six, with roll call and the raising of the flag. They breakfasted on bread and milk, and then each inmate went to work. The kitchen detail peeled potatoes and prepared the meat. Outdoor workers went out to the vegetable garden, and indoor workers began the tasks of maintenance and cleaning. After lunch, everyone rested before the kitchen detail returned at three to make dinner. They were allowed to work at crafts, so long as they avoided depicting symbols of peace or freedom, such as doves or horses.

Sara's favorite duty was in the garden, where in spite of everything, she found herself still capable of experiencing moments of pleasure—turning over the soil and planting seeds, watching them sprout, and studying the insects working alongside her.

She discovered that the women had a small library and studied together, each one teaching the others what she knew best—drawing, sewing, geography, physics—and that they shared the food and the money brought to them by their families. They were not allowed to have radios, newspapers, or magazines, so they devised other means of keeping themselves informed. Children, who weren't as closely watched as adults when they visited relatives, were taught to convey news through games and stories, and in this way, the women received a smattering of information about what was going on in the outside world.

As the day of her first family visit approached, Sara kept finding small, gray seeds on her pillow, in the book she was reading, inside a pocket. These seeds were much used in the making of rosaries and jewelry and she learned that long before she arrived, the women had chosen them as a symbol, a means of expressing support for one another. They meant simply, "We're with you." Sara treasured each one, as well as all the advice offered to her. She needed to be careful with her speech, they told her. If the guard assigned to stand by her during her visit suspected that forbidden information was being exchanged about the movements of subversives still on the loose, the visit would be cut short. The two burning questions she needed to ask—was Simón with her family, and where was Mauricio?—had to be asked and answered without revealing names.

She was a mass of nerves as the day finally arrived and she was ushered into the more secure of the two visitors' rooms. It was a large room, divided down the middle by a long table with wooden chairs on either side. Down the center of the table ran a thick pane of ceiling-high glass. Headphones hung at intervals down either side. There, his hands clasped on the table, his hair grayer and his face more deeply lined, sat her father. All the strength seemed to leave her body and her hands were sweating as she put on the headphones. How she longed to touch him, to feel the comfort of his embrace. Instead, they sat facing one another for a while, mirror images, not knowing what to say or how to say it.

"How are you, Sara?"

"Well. I am well. And *mamá?*"

"Very happy. She had been worried."

"I'm sorry."

"We're so glad that you're alive."

"And the others?"

"Everyone is well. Do you remember Uncle Julito?"

This must be a code he was establishing, Sara thought. "Yes. How is he?"

"He asked me to send you his love—from Spain—and tell you that he's had his hair cut very short. He said you'd laugh."

Was her father referring to Mauricio? "Is it still red?"

"Yes . . . but fading."

What was Mauricio doing in Spain? Had he taken Simón with him? "How is his son?"

"Well . . . I . . . he . . . he said you were the one who'd seen him most recently."

Sara was unable to utter another word for the remainder of the visit.

* * *

From then on, Sara described her family visits as "a torment." Longing intensely for news of Simón, she alternated between counting the days between visits and wishing for sanctions that would forbid them. She had scratched a small clear place on the white-washed window near her bed from which she could watch the street and the arrival of families on visiting days, and her heart ached whenever she saw her father, her mother, her brothers and sisters. Whenever she was under a sanction for some real or invented misdemeanor, they would be turned away, and Sara knew from the way her father put his arm around her mother that she was crying. When they were allowed in, their visits were agonizing. All of them were afraid of saying something that could be used against them or others, and Sara hated putting them through these ordeals. She had to trust that they were doing everything they could to find Simón and Mauricio, and wait.

* * *

Sara had been imprisoned for six months when, on April 30, 1977, the Mothers of the Plaza de Mayo began what would become a weekly walk around the square in front of the Presidential Palace in Buenos Aires. They carried pictures of their disappeared children, and on their heads they wore white handkerchiefs, symbolizing the cloth diapers the children had once worn.

Sensing that a group of grieving mothers might pose a public relations problem, the Minister of the Interior, General Albano Harguindeguy, agreed to meet with them a few days after the first demonstration. Three of the marchers, accompanied by one of the group's founders, Azuzena Villaflor, were ushered into a sumptuous office. The women were offered tea, which they declined. Azuzena wasted no time getting to the point. Their children, all in their late teens, twenties, and early thirties, had disappeared, and they wanted to know where they were.

"Ladies," the general said, smoothing the impeccable crease on his trouser leg, "these 'disappearances' as you call them, are the work of gangs over which I have no control."

"Forgive me, general," Azuzena said, "but if that's the case then perhaps you are ill-suited to carry out the duties of a general and a minister."

The general was unaccustomed to insubordination and was struck momentarily dumb. He lit a cigarette and attempted a smile. "We all know that we aren't talking about innocent young men and women going about their business in the service of our great country. If your children disappeared, ladies, perhaps it was because they thought it best to leave. My own niece—a rebellious young woman with her head full of foreign ideas—is in Mexico now. I noticed when I visited her there that quite a few of the young women whose relatives claimed were disappeared are working there—as prostitutes."

It was the women's turn to sit silently, trying to decide whether to swallow this insult or not.

"And our sons?" Azuzena asked in an icy voice.

The general laughed. "Boys will be boys! They've probably run off with some girl you wouldn't approve of! As soon as it's out of their systems, they'll be back, you'll see."

CHAPTER VI

Repression and death were underground phenomena ... Torture was real only in the physical and psychic traces left in the victims and their families.

THE LATIN AMERICAN INSTITUTE ON MENTAL HEALTH AND HUMAN RIGHTS.

S ara had been in solitary confinement for twenty-four hours, on bread and water. She had four weeks to go, plenty of time to dwell on the events that had landed her where she was, on the way the world outside appeared to be changing, and on how the two were connected. The British ambassador had paid a visit to Punta de Rieles. Great Britain was considering buying thousands of tons of frozen beef from Uruguay, and before the deal went through, the ambassador had been sent to see that the treatment in the women's prison was humane. Prisoners were lined up for his inspection and told to remain silent. Sara had disobeyed. She had stepped out of line, told the ambassador about Simón, and asked for his help in finding him. She was aware of the peril of drawing attention to herself. The ambassador's predecessor, Geoffrey Jackson, had been a prisoner of the Tupamaro's six years before, and as a former guerrilla she had shared in the responsibility of his kidnapping.

It was rumored that the ambassador's visit to Punta de Rieles was part of an effort on the part of US President Jimmy Carter and his European allies to persuade the regimes to hold elections. Sara remembered how, at the beginning of the decade, the Vatican had called for "a man prepared to embrace humanity in its entirety." At the time, it appeared to be a forlorn hope, and if she had been asked to guess from which part of the world such a leader might emerge, Sara would not have chosen the United States.

In January of 1977, however, James Earl Carter, Jr. had assumed the presidency of the United States, and for Latin Americans, the Vatican's call was met in full measure. It was clear from the beginning of his administration that President Carter's leadership would differ in significant ways from that of his predecessors. Instead of supporting them, Jimmy Carter brought all the power of his presidency to bear upon South American dictators, pressuring them to hold elections. The damage done to democracy by previous administrations was nevertheless so profound that when General Hugo Banzer of Bolivia responded to US pressure and announced that elections would be held in July of 1978, Bolivians were subjected to a series of military coups ending in the particularly corrupt and violent rule of General Luis García Meza, whose forces placed over two thousand people under arrest, while killing and "disappearing" hundreds more. Since military aid from the United States was no longer an option, Bolivia's *Junta* sought and found it from Argentina, which supplied its Condor Plan partner with tanks and communication equipment. President Carter responded by cutting off all aid to Bolivia, and again the Argentine *Junta* were quick to step in with eight hundred million dollars contributed toward "the fight against communism."

In Argentina, US Ambassador Robert Hill, previously sympathetic toward the *Junta,* was experiencing a change of heart. The son of an Argentine employee at the embassy had disappeared, and Hill, using his considerable influence, attempted to assist the family in locating the young man. His exalted position as United

States ambassador availed him little. His inquiries were dealt with in the same manner as the inquiries of thousands of other families and friends—no records could be found to attest to the young man's ever having passed through the hands of the authorities. Perhaps he had moved, they said. He would be in touch when he felt ready.

Inadvertently, President Jimmy Carter had gained an active, if deeply disillusioned supporter and the embassy proceeded to change in a number of ways. The ambassador's home was no longer surrounded by machine guns, and at the embassy itself a young diplomat who went by the name of "Tex" Harris opened the doors to anyone who wanted to see him. Tex was overwhelmed with requests for help and devoted every waking hour to helping the families of the disappeared, calling on them at their homes and gaining first-hand knowledge of what was really happening in Argentina.

* * *

Every inmate at the women's prison had her own way of dealing with solitary confinement. One woman had a book going in her head, to which she added a chapter every time she was in solitary; another, a former teacher, reviewed every fact she had ever learned and could remember.

Sara exercised. She could take two full steps in her cell, turn, and take two more. In this fashion she walked up to five kilometers a day. She also saved a small piece of bread from every portion given to her, shaped it and colored it with tooth paste until she had a complete chess set. By means of taps on the wall—one tap for A, two for B—she and the woman next door communicated the moves to one another.

When the bag containing her bedding and personal hygiene products was delivered to her, she opened it immediately, knowing that her cell mates would have been inventive in the ways they devised to include items that would help while away the hours. Worked into the thick side seam of her nightgown was a needle, and in the hem, several strands of colored thread. The buttons were sewn on with a large quantity of thread, none of it tied off, so she could unpick it, use it, and unpick it again.

Her fellow prisoners also did everything they could to make her feel less isolated. Whenever they were in the vicinity of the solitary confinement cells they raised their voices, or whistled a favorite tune. Those on cleaning duty went as close as they dared to the cells and tried to exchange a few words with the women inside, knowing that for many the fear of going insane in solitary was always present. They hoped for what they called "cell dreams," which were not nightmares, but good dreams, full of light, animals, fields, and freedom. They left the dreamer with a feeling of hope that made the following day bearable. Sara enjoyed these dreams when they came, but not because she feared madness. For her, insanity was not an option so long as her son Simón was missing.

* * *

In 1978 Argentina would host the World Cup, and no expense was being spared to clean up the country and its image. Burson Marstellar, a New York company, had been hired to coordinate the effort. While Buenos Aires was being given a face-lift and all evidence of their existence kept under tighter wraps than ever, the imprisoned Argentines and Uruguayans at Orletti and other holding centers continued to tap messages to one another through the damp and peeling walls.

In the United States, Henry Kissinger, who was to be a guest of honor at the events, maintained that the Argentine *Junta* was doing the best it could. The fact that they were using an iron fist to control terrorism should not be allowed to interfere with any business decisions being made by either country. David Rockefeller agreed. The Chase Manhattan Bank, of which he was President, was among those that had lent the *Junta* money at rates exceeding the prime rate. Senator Edward Kennedy's was one of the few voices raised in Congress protesting a private practice that undermined the goals and intentions of US public policy, and he supported President Carter's intention to block future loans to the regime.

When Argentina's team made its way to the finals and emerged victorious winners of the World Cup, Burson Marstellar's public relations bill—five hundred million dollars—was considered cheap at the price.

In the United States during the course of that same year, war industry suppliers were becoming increasingly vocal in their complaints that human rights sanctions prevented them from selling arms and supplies to the dictatorships of Latin America. Patricia Derian, Assistant Secretary of State for Human Rights, was being ridiculed in the press for her outspoken criticism of torture and disappearances. General Gordon Sumner, Jr., who would become a special advisor to Ronald Reagan on Latin American affairs, declared that only communists and those who wished to destroy the American way of life derived any benefit from President Carter's position on human rights.

In Uruguay, the joint military and police forces had grown by 22,000 since 1970 to a total of 64,000, all of them requiring weapons being mass-produced in the United States. This figure represented one policeman or military personnel per fifty inhabitants,

In 1979 a meeting was arranged between General Videla and Vice President Walter Mondale. Mondale agreed to see what he could do to free up the money President Carter was unwilling to lend the regime, if Videla allowed the Organization of American

States' (OAS) Inter American Commission for Human Rights to inspect certain sites. One of them was the Navy Mechanics School, ESMA, out of which a secret detention center was known to operate, with its accompanying extermination camp. General Videla agreed to the inspection, but before the OAS set foot in the school, most of the prisoners were transferred to an island in the Tigre River. In spite of everything the *Junta* did to impede their investigation, in April of 1980 the OAS delegation released its report. There could no longer be any question that torture was routinely practiced in Argentina and that thousands of disappeared persons had been murdered.

The *Junta* was undaunted. Two months later, Peruvian Army Intelligence kidnapped four Argentines living in exile in Peru. One of them was a member of the Mothers of the Plaza de Mayo. Her body was found one month later—in Madrid.

August of 1980 brought the Fourth Congress of the Latin American Anti Communist Confederation to Buenos Aires. Presiding over the event was Argentine General Carlos Suárez Mason. Among those attending were assistants to Republican Senators Jesse Helms and James McClure. The Congress condemned "Carter's Communism," and asked that Latin America follow the example of eighteenth-century Spain by ordering a second expulsion of the Jesuits—also accused of being communists—from the Southern continent.

In an attempt to persuade the Carter administration of their good intentions, the *Junta* released a few prisoners—among them Carla and Fernando.

Their sons Gabriel and Daniel were four and three years old, and the entire family, parents, aunts, uncles, and the children, went to Argentina to celebrate and see them off to Belgium, where they had been offered asylum. The only one who couldn't participate in the festivities was Elena, who knew that as soon as Carla and Fernando were settled in Brussels they would want their sons back. Relations between Elena and Carla were strained further when it became obvious that the boys, confronted by parents who were essentially strangers to them, clung to Elena. It was no use telling Carla that she had done her best to explain to the boys that she was not their mother. Carla cringed every time one of her sons said *"mamá"* and it was not directed at her. She kept telling them that she would be sending for them soon and they would all live together, but that only upset the boys more, and Elena did not know how to comfort them.

The next few months were heart-rending for Elena. She would be playing with Gabriel and Daniel in the park, or picking them up at nursery school and all she could think was that soon it would be the last time. When the dreaded moment arrived, it was all she could do not to break down in front of the boys. She left it to her husband Antonio to pack their clothes and toys, but as she watched him she could not hold back. He had put Gabriel's favorite car in the suitcase instead of leaving it out for him to play with on the long plane ride, and she had to rescue a tattered book from the garbage and explain to Antonio that it was the book she read to Daniel every night.

Watching them walk away from her at the airport she felt as if a piece was being torn out of her, and for several days she could hardly bear to be in the apartment or go anywhere they had gone together. Her son Andrés also reacted strongly to his cousins' departure. He became listless and apathetic, didn't want to eat, and cried at the slightest provocation. Antonio's cousin Paco recommended taking him to a play-group, and after that Andrés began to improve. There was no such remedy for Elena; she had to trust to time to ease her pain.

* * *

Following an unsuccessful attempt to rescue fifty-two US citizens being held hostage by Ayatollah Khomeini in Teheran, Ronald Reagan defeated Jimmy Carter in the presidential elections. No one celebrated with more glee than the Condor Plan partners.

The new Secretary of State, Alexander Haig, let Argentina know that it would receive no more public reproaches for its human rights abuses. The newly-established friendship between the two nations would lead to several illegal activities, including a US arms transfer to Iran, and an agreement reached with CIA Director William Casey that the US would provide the money and Argentina the training for the Nicaraguan *contras* organizing to bring down the government there.

There were nevertheless those in Congress who continued to confront the *Junta*. Democrat Senator Claiborne Pell asked General Roberto Viola, Argentine Army Chief of Staff, when the general planned to keep his promise of publishing a list of the disappeared. Viola's response was printed in the newspaper *Clarín* on March 18, 1981. "I think you are suggesting that we investigate the Security Forces—that is absolutely out of the question. This is a war and we are the winners. You can be certain that in the last war if the armies of the Reich had won, the war crimes trials would have taken place in Virginia, not in Nuremberg." General Viola was among newly elected President Reagan's first official visitors.

In spite of unrelenting repression and losing their strongest United States ally, Jimmy Carter, Argentines continued to demand elections, and fifteen thousand of them gathered at a protest in the Plaza de Mayo on March 31, 1982. By this time, the Mothers of the Plaza de Mayo Association, denounced by the military as being financed by terrorists, was drawing ten thousand supporters to its weekly marches. A few days after the March protest, following an age-old stratagem used to distract the populace from focusing on serious issues at home, Argentina embarked on a war, challenging Great Britain for possession of the Falkland (or Malvinas) Islands in the Straits of Magellan. Occupied and administered by Britain as a British crown colony since 1833, the Falkland Islands comprise about 200 islands totaling approximately 4,700 square miles. The human population numbered about 2,700, with the addition of many thousands of sheep.

The distraction worked, especially when—in spite of some powerful allies in Washington—Congress came down on Great Britain's side, not Argentina's, effectively leaving Argentina to fight alone. Fed by a massive public relations campaign, orchestrated by the military, patriotic furor reached an all-time high.

For the seventy-two days of the war's duration, the Argentine people were misinformed about the outcome of battles and confrontations, believing that their forces were beating the Britons. Following the surrender of the Argentines on South Georgia Island, it was revealed that not only were the military masters of misinformation, they had been totally humiliated on the field of battle. Ten thousand of them were taken prisoner, making Argentina's national shame complete. Six hundred and fifty-five Argentines lost their lives in the effort, and two hundred and thirty-six Britons. Costs were estimated at two billion dollars.

While still trying to make sense of and recover from what had happened to them during the Falkland Islands War, Argentines began to hear about hundreds of unidentified bodies turning up in local cemeteries. The promise made to the shocked and dismayed population by the new head of the *Junta*, that elections would be held in two years-time, went almost unnoticed.

Along with public trust, another casualty of the war was the economy. The Argentine *peso* was devalued, a move that immediately affected Uruguay, heavily dependent on Argentina not only for tourism dollars, but for real estate investments. Both countries went into an economic recession, and Uruguay's burden of debt grew even heavier, from $515 million in 1976 to three billion by 1982, a significant figure for a population of less than four million people to attempt to repay.

* * *

Sara was thirty-seven when she was released from prison in May of 1981. Shortly after her release, she received the bill for the costs incurred for her imprisonment. They included food, lodging, security, and medical expenses. The total amount was the equivalent of a year's teaching salary. She was also notified that she would have to present herself at military headquarters every two weeks and could not leave Montevideo without permission.

Mauricio telephoned her and urged her to join him in Spain. Sara had heard from other exiled friends that he had had several relationships with other women there, which Mauricio defended by saying that they had all been contingent upon Sara's release. Hearing his voice left her cold. How could he think that she would leave Uruguay with Simón still missing?

Sara took to walking along the *Rambla* for several hours every day, thinking of everything the river had provided throughout her life—a place to play and swim; rocks among which to hide and read; fish to eat; driftwood to burn, shells and feathers to collect; the sound of waves on the shore, the feel of sand beneath bare feet, the sight of the sky streaked in pink and lavender at sunset. Never further than a walk or short bus ride away, the river soothed the senses and shut out the noises of the city, allowing her to feel in touch with nature. Sara had always derived strength from the Río de la Plata's mighty presence, a strength she sorely needed now as she looked for a means of support and of paying back the money she owed for her imprisonment.

She went to work in the accounting department of a factory,

finding it beneficial to have something other than her quest for Simón to occupy her mind for several hours of the day.

Her first step in locating her son was to request a meeting with the head of the Office of Disappeared Persons at the Ministry of Defense, Lieutenant Colonel Maynard. Maynard asked for proof that Simón had been born and abducted before he was a month old. Sara had none. Simón's birth certificate had been left in the house with him. Who knew what had become of it? As for Simón being abducted, Maynard warned Sara that if she kept harping on that story, she would be sent back to jail. It was Sara's first official indication that not only would she receive no help from the military in her search for Simón, there would also be no acknowledgement of his existence, let alone his disappearance.

She learned that the families of the disappeared were organizing themselves into a unit in order to pursue information about their missing relatives. All of them had met with the same response Maynard had given Sara. What evidence did they have that their sons and daughters had disappeared? The fact that they were missing was not enough. Unable to get a hearing at home, they created SERPAJ, the Service for Peace and Justice, and began collecting facts about the disappeared for dissemination abroad. Sara also became involved with Families of the Detained Disappeared, and attended functions held by Families of Political Prisoners. All of these groups were closely watched, and characterized by the military as communist efforts to continue organizing resistance groups.

Not only was Sara putting in very long days between her job and her involvement with the families of the disappeared, but she also found herself becoming a symbol of hope for many who believed that their loved ones hadn't been killed, that they were being held somewhere, perhaps in some forgotten prison, and would one day show up, just as Sara had. As soon as democracy returned to South America, they would all be found and they could pick up the pieces of their lives and move on. Sara walked a fine line between nurturing hope and feeling unable to say that that hope was misguided.

She had imagined that finding Simón would be a matter of following through on every lead she could unearth, a task she would approach systematically, like a detective. Except that she didn't know where to start. She had hung on to the hope that Simón had been put in an orphanage, but as she knew from Violeta and Ester, and countless others who had searched orphanages, there were no records of such children, or if there were, they were not being made available.

Two years dragged by with no leads concerning Simón's fate.

* * *

The only bright spot for Uruguay during this time was that, following a decade of union repression, a collective bargaining law was approved. On May 1, 1983—International Workers Day—one hundred and fifty thousand people participated in a rally. It was nothing compared to the rally that followed. Organized by revitalized political parties and various social groups pledging support for democracy, it was named "the river of freedom." Four hundred thousand people turned out onto the streets of Montevideo to protest the dictatorship. The military recognized that the tide was turning irrevocably against them and began taking small steps to prepare for elections.

In Argentina, elections were held on October 30, 1983. Presidential candidate Raúl Alfonsín Foulkes was not expected to win. He was running on a platform promising prosecution of those responsible for the horrors the country had endured, and his opponent was a member of the Peronist party that had dominated Argentine politics since the 1940s. But win he did and one of the guests of honor at the inaugural ceremony was Patricia Derian, former Assistant Secretary of State for Human Rights during the Carter administration. The following year, former President Carter himself paid a visit to Argentina, and the *Buenos Aires Herald* greeted him simply with the headline: Gracias, Jimmy. "Jimmy Carter's administration," the *Herald* said, "did more than anyone anywhere for human rights in Argentina."

Three guests were booed during President Alfonsín's inauguration. They were the representatives of the dictatorships of Uruguay and Chile, and the former head of the CIA, who was at the time Vice President of the United States, George H.W. Bush.

President Alfonsín was even-handed in allocating responsibility for the acts of terrorism that had occurred during the previous decade. One of his first official acts was the establishment of an independent commission charged with investigating the disappeared. He followed it up by prosecuting several of the guerrilla leaders.

Economically, Argentina's new administration faced a daunting challenge. The national debt was five times what it had been before the military takeover, and the country had suffered a massive brain drain. Alfonsín wanted the banks that had made the loans leading to the national debt to share in the responsibility by forgiving a percentage of what was owed. Led by Donald Regan, US Secretary of the Treasury, those banks instead called for austerity and increased lending.

In March of 1984, after spending over eight years in prison, the head of Uruguay's new Frente Amplio, former General Liber Seregni Mosquera, was released. It is not unusual in Latin America for high-ranking members of the military to run in elections. Typically, they represent the "constitutional military" and are defenders of democracy and the democratic process.

Lest General Seregni's release should raise any false hopes, the

Junta made it clear that he was forbidden from running for public office.

Three months later, on June 16, Wilson Ferreira Aldunate, head of Uruguay's National (Blanco) Party, returned from eleven years living in exile. He was allowed to enter Uruguay, and promptly arrested, another not-so-subtle message that the *Junta* would be determining the conditions of a return to democracy. Uruguay's response to Ferreira Aldunate's arrest was to call a general strike for June 27, the eleventh anniversary of the military takeover. Knowing that their days were numbered, the *Junta* began negotiations with the other two major contenders—the *Colorado* and *Frente Amplio* parties. The *Blanco* party was invited to participate in these discussions, but they declined so long as their leader, Ferreira Aldunate, remained in jail. Plans for holding elections went ahead without the *Blancos*, who refused to be on the ballot without Ferreira Aldunate. Elections were held in Uruguay in November of 1984. The *Colorados* won, and Ferreira Aldunate was released on December 5, five days after the closing of the polls.

Hope ran high in Uruguay regarding a proposal to grant general amnesty to all political prisoners and to those exiled as a result of their political activities. Perhaps, people said, everyone could just admit that regrettable mistakes had been made on both sides, but that in a country the size of Uruguay it would be best to exercise the spirit of good sportsmanship, shake hands, and move on.

Discussions about granting amnesty to the military were also ongoing. The amnesty proposed forgiving crimes committed by the Armed Forces and the police from the time a state of internal warfare was declared in 1972 until a democratic government took over in March of 1985. An exception would be made for homicide. Any member of the Armed Forces or police accused of homicide would be tried by a military court, with the possibility of appeal to the country's Supreme Court.

Opposition to the military amnesty measure was strong, and many called for a referendum on the issue, among them Sara and Ester. Amnesty would make it impossible to compel Gavazzo and others like him to tell what they knew about Simón, about Emilia, Jorge and Mariana.

The military argued that it would be unfair to forgive the crimes committed on one side, while holding the other side accountable. The Tupamaros in turn claimed that they had already served their time, spending years in prison, where they endured beatings and torture that in some cases permanently impaired their physical and psychic health, while the military had not been called upon to account in any way for their actions.

Amnesty for political prisoners and for those exiled as a result of their political activities was approved in spite of the military's objections, and soon close to four hundred suits relating to the disappeared were filed in court. With thousands of exiles returning home, the courts anticipated the filing of hundreds more.

* * *

Never one to be idle, Ester became actively involved in assisting people to file legal suits against the military before amnesty was granted to them for their crimes.

It was almost like old times, Ester thought. Violeta's family gathered for Sunday lunch, all of them a little older, a little thinner, a little sadder, but alive, which was more than could be said for many other families, including her own.

Neither Ester nor Violeta had been aware that Violeta's son-in-law Sergio, now an army captain, would be there, or Violeta would not have invited Ester. Their friendship was surviving despite the profound difference in their circumstances. Violeta's daughter Carla and her husband Fernando were safely in exile with their two children, while no trace had been found of Emilia, Jorge or Mariana.

Ester did not believe that Sergio himself was responsible for the disappearance of women and children in Buenos Aires, but neither was he among the military men who called for an investigation into the actions of his colleagues. In fact, he was unhappy at the turn events were taking. "They released all the prisoners!" he said. "No matter who they had killed, what they had done, nothing. Amnesty for everybody! Where's the fairness in letting them out, and wanting to hold us accountable?"

"The Tupas served their time," Violeta's son Alejandro said. "They spent years in prison, they were beaten up, tortured—"

"We never tortured anybody!" Sergio said.

"Yes, yes, we know. They came out crippled and crazy from some strange disease only Tupas suffer from!"

Violeta's face was a study in anguish. Short of forbidding them to speak, she didn't know what to say to steer the conversation away from the subject of amnesty.

"Show me one cripple," Sergio said, "one crazy who wasn't crazy before he went in! I'm not saying we didn't put pressure on people to obtain information. There were times when we knew they were going to wipe out one of ours, we didn't know where, and we needed to know, so—"

"So you tortured them?" said Alejandro.

"We pressured them! They'd better give us amnesty as well, or—"

"Or what, you'll come back?" *don* Ramón asked.

"The country could do worse! Politicians are a disaster when it comes to ruling a country."

"That may be the only thing you and I will ever agree on, Sergio," Alejandro said. "I think they'll cave, as they always do, and they'll give you your amnesty."

"Zero to zero and the ball to the center!"

"So, everyone should just be a good loser, take their ball, and go home?"

"That is the Uruguayan tradition!"

"This isn't a soccer match! What has been lost isn't a game between evenly matched teams."

"There were truly innocent victims, Sergio," *don* Ramón said. "Even you can't blame Mariana for what happened to her."

"Of course not. But that didn't happen here."

Ester could control herself no longer. "I am so tired of hearing that." she said. "When will you admit that you were involved?"

"He wasn't involved!" Josefina said. "How dare you accuse my husband of such a thing!"

"Perhaps he never tortured anyone, never took a child and gave it away, but if he doesn't know his friend Nino Gavazzo did just that, then either he's a liar or an idiot!"

For a brief second there was silence. Everyone was shocked that the argument had escalated to such a pitch.

Ester got up. "I'm sorry. Please forgive me for spoiling your lunch."

Violeta and *don* Ramón got up with her. "I'm so sorry, Ester," Violeta said.

Hearing her mother apologize was too much for Josefina.

"You criticize Nino when Emi and Jorge and their friends executed people—here, where the death penalty was abolished decades ago! They kidnapped people, kept them in subhuman conditions, shot poor defenseless policemen and soldiers in a pre-meditated, planned, and yes, treasonous manner."

"I would prefer," Sergio added, "being an idiot or a liar to being a murderer or a traitor!"

"Do you want to know where the difference lies?" Ester shot back. "You were charged with upholding the law! You had the power and the choice to do it! And you failed! You talk of treason? What can be more treasonous than to betray the Constitution you swore to uphold?"

Before another word could be spoken, Ester left. Violeta followed her outside and they threw their arms around each other, determined that the world all around them might unravel, but the weave of their old friendship would not.

* * *

With the threat of military intervention hanging over them, by the end of the year the Uruguayan Parliament was ready to act. On December 22, 1985, a law was passed making it impossible to bring anything other than a civil suit against those who had carried out their duties in the name of the State.

Sara was invited to testify at the Legal and Social Studies Center in Buenos Aires. Under President Alfonsín, the Center had begun gathering information for legal proceedings against the former dictators. As someone who had survived Orletti, Sara was a key witness. She decided to risk a breach of her parole by taking a trip to Buenos Aires. While she was there, she would also visit the Mothers of the Plaza de Mayo.

She decided to travel through the coastal town of Colonia, knowing she was less likely to be stopped there. She was nervous as she approached customs and her heart sank when her documents were examined and she was asked to step into a small office. While she was waiting, she thrust her hands in her pockets and tried to shred all the little papers on which she had listed the telephone numbers she would need in Buenos Aires. When the official who had detained her returned, he was apologetic.

"An old detention order was still on file—from 1973! We're very sorry for having bothered you, *señora*. You're free to board."

Unbelievable, Sara thought, relief flooding through her. The bureaucracy had managed to unearth a document a decade old and overlooked the other one issued when she was released from prison, stating that she could not travel without official approval. Before she boarded the ferry for Buenos Aires, she ran into the bathroom and tried to piece together the scraps of paper she had shredded. There was only one telephone number she could still read, and it would have to do. She would use it to get to the others.

She checked into the Buenos Aires YWCA, dropped off her small suitcase, and took a bus that left her a block from the house from which she had been taken seven years before. The front door had long since been repaired, and the façade boasted a fresh coat of white paint. If only the house could talk, tell her what had happened to Simón after she was taken away.

She and Mauricio had barely known their neighbors. When she rang the doorbell of the house next door, a woman she didn't recognize answered. Sara introduced herself and asked about the former tenant.

"She moved years ago."

"Do you know her address?"

"She went to Italy, to live with relatives, that's all I know."

Sara tried the house on the other side. The people living there were also unfamiliar, the former tenants killed in a car accident.

The cafes where she had met friends and the family markets where she and Mauricio had shopped were still there, but she recognized no one in them.

Sara was unprepared for the emotions that assailed her in the city where she had loved Mauricio and given birth to Simón. Everywhere she went was a reminder of times she had spent with Emilia and Carla, of their children, of Gerardo and Jorge and Fernando, of Mauricio—all dead or exiled now. Why, Sara wondered? Why had some of them been spared and others taken?

There seemed no rhyme or reason to any of it.

At the Legal and Social Studies Center, they were waiting for her with a tape recorder. She was made comfortable in a small office, given coffee and water, and asked if she would record everything she remembered about her life in Buenos Aires, the night she was taken, the days she spent at Orletti, and her transfer to Montevideo.

As she began telling her story, she realized it was the first time she had told it all. She had recounted bits and pieces to her family, to friends, to her prison companions—but she had never sat down and told the whole story from beginning to end. Now, the tape recorder kept malfunctioning, recording for a while, and then leaving blanks on the tape, so Sara had to keep going back and repeating her story. Every time she did, details became clearer, odd bits and pieces surfaced, like seeing herself in Gavazzo's dark glasses, the smell of gasoline at Orletti, the radio programs her captors favored.

The painfully cathartic experience left her exhausted. But after a good night's sleep—just as she had felt a surge of energy at the prospect of facing torture—she plowed ahead now with her search for Simón. Her hopes were high as she proceeded to the headquarters of the Mothers of the Plaza de Mayo—now a fully-fledged, legal association, with premises and a staff of volunteers. If anyone could help her to find Simón it was these persistent, undaunted women, credited with having played a significant role in the downfall of the Argentine military and instrumental in leading the effort to reunite missing children with their families.

Sara was warmly received at the headquarters, and the organization's files were made available to her. As she was preparing to get down to work, she saw a middle-aged woman dressed in black standing by a display cabinet containing a worn blanket and a vest, her hand resting caressingly on the glass. Sara approached her and saw that it was Blanca Artigas, who she had met at several meetings of the families of the disappeared in Montevideo. Sara put her arm around her. Blanca turned, her face lighting up as she recognized Sara.

"See the vest, Sara? Read what the card says."

Mary gave me this vest in the Banfield concentration camp in July of '78, a few days after I arrived. It was my sole garment for eighty days. She taught me to roll bread into balls we could use for coloring. We made colors from bits of beet and other food scraps. Neither Mary nor her daughter has been found. I am leaving this vest with the Mothers. Yes, as a testimony, with memories of blood and tears. But also with hope, because even in the pits where they tried to silence us, life struggled on, and our solidarity survived. This vest then, is both a small and a great piece of solidarity.

"Did you know that Mary was held at the Pozo de Banfield and that she gave birth to a little girl there?" Blanca asked Sara. "Five years ago someone called to tell me."

"An anonymous call?" Sara asked.

"Oh, yes. In those days, you know . . ."

Sara did know. She had made such calls herself, passing along bits of information to desperate relatives.

Sara remembered Mary and her husband Fredi very well. Like Carla, they had harbored dozens of refugees, and the United Nations had offered them asylum abroad. Mary could not bear to go too far from her mother and father, or to leave the graves of two children she had buried in Buenos Aires. One had died of whooping cough, the other was a stillbirth. In a cruel twist of fate, Mary's only surviving child had been born and survived the worst of circumstances in the Banfield Pit, and was now lost.

Blanca was as determined as Sara never to give up looking for Mary, her husband Fredi, and their child. She had searched all the orphanages, marched with the Mothers, and had Mary's picture published in the papers. The result was that a woman called Elena, who had been at Banfield with Mary, had contacted the Mothers. Blanca asked Sara to join her at a meeting with Elena scheduled for that day, and Sara said she would do so gladly.

Before Elena arrived, the Mothers encouraged Blanca to let Elena tell her story at her own pace. It often happened that in reliving their experiences, witnesses broke down and were unable to continue. They might have to arrange several meetings before Blanca could ask all her questions.

Banfield had been one of over three hundred secret detention centers operating in Argentina, and it had been common for pregnant women to be sent there. When Elena contacted the Mothers, she told them she had been with Mary while she was pregnant.

As soon as Sara saw Elena, she thought that Blanca might not have to wait long for her answers. Elena was a slight woman, with an air of strength and determination. She hugged Blanca and said she had no objection to Sara being present—or anyone else who wanted to hear what had gone on at Banfield.

Elena began by telling them that the holding areas were dark and dank, shared by two to four prisoners. They were let out to eat only once every couple of days, and their toilets had consisted of bottles of bleach with the tops cut off. Being pregnant did not mean that Mary was spared from torture or interrogations, although they were more careful with her than they were with the others.

"How much do you want to know?" she asked Blanca.

"Everything. I want to know it all."

"We were beaten regularly, but in Mary's case the blows were restricted to her legs, and after a man came to confirm that she was pregnant, electricity was no longer used on her."

There had been one small window in the cell, and the two of them had taken turns lifting each other up to look out. They were in a residential area, about three stories up, and could see children playing soccer in an empty lot nearby.

"We developed our own Morse code and tapped messages to the others. Pieces of plaster were always falling off the ceiling. We used them to draw a chess board on the wall. We didn't have anything for pieces, so we held all the moves in our head. When we were hungry—which was almost all the time—we exchanged recipes." Elena smiled. "I still use the one Mary said was your specialty—*pascualina*. My neighbors tell me I make the best spinach pie in Montevideo!"

Elena and Mary had told one another of places they had traveled to, remembered their old neighborhoods, and shared family stories. "I probably know as much about you as your own family does, *señora* Blanca!"

One day, Elena said, when Mary was feeling very down, they'd agreed to "go out."

"We drew the streets of the neighborhood where we had both lived—the plaza, every shop and restaurant. Then we visited every one of them and all the benches in the plaza, every tree and flower bed. She told me that you have a green thumb and that anything you plant flourishes! I know you are longing to hear about the baby, but I'm telling you all this so that you'll know that Mary wasn't alone, that she had people who loved her, even in Banfield."

Elena accepted the coffee the Mothers offered before going on with her story. "When Mary went into labor, I kept track of her contractions by making a mark on the wall for every minute that passed between them. And I tapped the information to our companions in the cell behind ours so they could keep track too, in case I made a mistake. When the contractions were five minutes apart, I called the guards and they took her away."

"Did you see her again? Did you see the baby?"

"I never saw the baby, but I did see Mary. She came back later that night. She had given birth in another cell, a little less dark than ours and with a sheet on the floor. Her handcuffs had been taken off and she'd been given a lot of forms to fill out, with her name, and Fredi's, and all their medical history. And the name they chose for their child—María Victoria"

"The birth had gone well?"

"They had a doctor there to assist her. She was blindfolded, so she couldn't see him, but he let her have the baby for an hour before he took her away. He told Mary not to breastfeed her, but Mary did anyway."

"That's my girl!"

They had come to the difficult part of the story, and for the first time Elena hesitated. "I don't know much more, *señora* Blanca. I was released a few weeks later, and it was my husband who called you to tell you that Veronica had been born. We left the country after that and have only recently returned."

"And the vest?" Blanca asked.

"It was Mary's. Until she heard that a young man was being held naked. Then she gave it to him."

"Tell Blanca what you told us, Elena," the Mothers said. "About Oscar Penna."

"Oscar Penna was in charge at Banfield, and it was he who brought a man to see Mary while she was pregnant. I think if you can find Penna, you may be able to find out what happened to Mary and Veronica."

* * *

Sara began work on the files, which she was disappointed to find consisted of only three file cabinets, one for boys, one for girls, and a third for miscellaneous information concerning them. Sara opened the boy's file cabinet and saw a row of folders, some slim, some overflowing, arranged haphazardly in the drawers. An effort had been made to organize the material chronologically and alphabetically, but often all a folder contained was a rumor, a suspicion, or a random fact.

"We do our best," the woman helping her said, "but we're all volunteers. Most of us have no training in keeping records."

Determined not to miss any clue, however small or hidden, that could help her find Simón, Sara began the laborious process of going through the files one piece of paper at a time. On the following day, she was hard at work when the president of the organization, María Isabel Chrobik de Mariani, known as Chicha, arrived at headquarters. Chicha was an energetic, middle-aged woman, with strong features and a direct gaze. She was elegant in the way of many Argentine women, dressed in a well-cut, simple silk dress accented by a plain gold necklace. Chicha introduced herself to Sara and welcomed her warmly, asking if she was receiving all the help she needed. Sara assured her that everyone at the center had been most helpful. Chicha then asked questions about her search, assuming that, like most of the women who came to them for help, Sara was looking for an adult son or daughter. When she heard about Simón, and Sara's description of him, Chicha surprised Sara by inviting her to accompany her directly to her house.

On the way, Chicha told Sara that in the early days, when they had had to operate secretly and couldn't keep records, she wrote down the pieces of information that came to her and put them in tin cans, which she buried in her back garden.

"I wish I had thought of that," Sara said, remembering the files in her makeshift code.

"Were you keeping records too?"

"Mainly of Uruguayans disappearing here. I kept notes, articles that appeared in the foreign press, that kind of thing."

"What became of them?"

"I don't know. They were in the house when I was taken."

"Were they in code?"

"Yes. My own, very crude."

"Do you remember any of the facts?"

"Some."

"Would you write them down for us?"

"Of course."

When they arrived at Chicha's house, she ushered Sara in, found two pairs of old shoes and trousers they could wear, and took her out to the back garden.

"For years," Chicha said, "I could have told you exactly where everyone was. Now I remember only a few. Next to the fig tree there's information about little twin brothers. Under that rose bush there's something about a three-year-old girl. In the end there were so many tins. In one of them, there's information about a red-headed baby. We'll dig until we find it!" Chicha handed Sara a spade, took one for herself, and they went to work in the flower beds and under the trees. Every time a tin surfaced, Chicha greeted it like an old friend, looked inside, and put it by the fig tree. The information the tins contained might prove useful, and she would have one of the volunteers enter it in the files.

By the end of the afternoon, they had unearthed thirty-five tins, none with information about a red-headed baby. But Chicha was not easily defeated. They would start spreading the word, and soon information would surface, she guaranteed it. Sara was not to despair. They were committed to finding every one of the disappeared and would not stop until they did.

"Tell me about the father. Who was he?" Chicha asked as they washed their hands and changed their clothes. When she learned that Mauricio was alive and in Spain, had suffered three heart attacks, and was facing a bypass operation, she told Sara not to waste a moment. Before he underwent surgery, Mauricio should have blood drawn and deposited in a genetic data bank in

Argentina, against the day when it would be needed to determine Simón's identity.

CHAPTER VII

First, we'll kill the subversives. Then the collaborators. Then the sympathizers. Then the undecided. And finally, we'll kill the indifferent.

ARGENTINE GENERAL IBÉRICO SAINT-JEAN

F or Ester, eight years had now gone by with no news of Emilia, Jorge, and Mariana. Little hope remained that the adults would be found alive, and Ester shifted her focus to confirming their deaths. And to looking for Mariana.

Violeta was in her garden pruning her roses when Ester came hurrying down the street brandishing a newspaper. She opened the front gate and sat on the low front wall. "Have you seen today's paper?" she asked breathlessly.

"Not yet," Violeta said, sitting by Ester and wiping her hands.

"A Brazilian journalist got an interview with one of Argentina's intelligence officers, and he talked! Anonymously of course. He revealed that a couple had been processed at his base. An Uruguayan couple, with a daughter Mariana's age. Someone at the base adopted the child, the man said. He was describing Emi and Jorge and Mariana, I know it!"

"Is it possible?"

"Who else do we know who fits the description? Uruguayans. A girl child. The right age. I am going to São Paulo!"

"To do what?"

"To interview the bastard myself!"

* * *

Standing outside the premises of the Brazilian newspaper *O Estado de São Paulo,* Ester's courage momentarily failed her. Reporters were notorious for not revealing their sources. What had made her imagine they would deviate from that rule for her? She hadn't come this far to turn back, however, so she took herself in hand and marched into the paper's offices, requesting to see the editor. She was asked her business. She stated it simply. "I am a mother and grandmother of the disappeared."

A few minutes later, she was seated in the editor's office.

"*Señora,*" the soft-spoken Brazilian said, "you understand of course that we cannot reveal our source."

"I don't need his name."

"But you want us to arrange an interview?"

Ester took a photo of Mariana out of her purse and handed it to him. "This is the granddaughter I'm looking for."

The editor looked at the photo for several long seconds, then sighed and reached for the phone.

* * *

The next day, Ester found herself participating in what felt like an undercover operation. She had been instructed to take a round-about route to the Blue Tavern Restaurant. She was to ask for a cup of coffee and wait. The Argentine agent had been provided with her description. If he felt it safe to do so, he would approach her. Ester followed the instructions to the letter. Her hand was steady as she poured sugar into her coffee and glanced quickly round the restaurant. Most of the lunchtime clientele had left. Only two other customers lingered over coffee and newspapers. Ester sensed rather than saw someone approach her.

"You are *Señora* de Islas?"

"Yes."

He was a pleasant looking man, clean shaven and neatly dressed in a linen suit. He asked for permission to sit. Ester gestured to the chair across from her. The waiter approached and the man ordered coffee and a ham and cheese sandwich. "Would you care for something to eat?" he asked politely.

Ester shook her head. "No, thank you."

As soon as the waiter left, Ester faced him squarely. "You know why I'm here."

"Oh, yes." He leaned forward, resting his elbows on the table. "I was fifteen when I joined the navy, you know. I never imagined that one day I would be fighting guerrillas like your daughter and son-in-law. They had the effrontery to call *us* ruthless! Did they ever tell you how they kidnapped people, held them for ransom, bombed us, shot soldiers? All in a country that gave them refuge when they needed it! They didn't believe in repaying kindness with kindness, it seems."

"They were idealists. They thought they were fighting for a good cause," Ester said, not wanting to antagonize him further.

"I was an idealist too when I joined up. If I hadn't been, I would have chosen a profession where I could get rich. Instead, I chose to serve my country."

"Unquestioningly?"

"I was educated to carry out orders, to apply my intellect, to carry them out within the parameters indicated by my superiors."

"What if your superiors ordered you to do immoral things?"

"One cannot have individuals making value judgments during a war! It would be chaos. Duty is a religion. When simple, courageous men go into combat they aren't interested in complex ideas, they ask only for an image, a symbol, a chief to follow. That chief must be a sort of god of war, a spiritual father, and a magnificent warrior. He must be capable of resolving any problem and leading his men to victory."

His coffee and sandwich arrived. They both waited until the waiter had left before Ester resumed the conversation.

"But if the orders are in conflict with your personal moral values, what then?"

"Then the soldier has a choice. Follow the orders anyway or abandon his training and become a pariah among those he has been conditioned to regard as his extended, and sometimes only, family."

"Do you have a family?"

"A wife and three daughters."

"Then you must understand how I feel."

"Like all those soldiers' mothers who also lost sons in this conflict."

"Surely you see the difference."

"The difference, *señora,* is that military men are trained to fight a conventional war, where both sides follow the rules. A guerrilla war is not like that."

"And that justifies the disappearance of children?"

"They didn't disappear, only their identity did. They are living another life, within another family."

"Is that what happened to my granddaughter?"

"I don't know if she was your granddaughter."

Ester pulled out the photograph she had shown to the editor. It was the last photo she had of Mariana, at eighteen months. In the photo, Mariana looks off to one side, her gaze direct, serious, questioning, as if she waits for someone. She is a beautiful baby, with large round eyes, and wisps of hair curling on her forehead. She is wearing tiny gold earrings and a dress with a high neck. There is an expectant, almost melancholy appeal to the photo that makes it compelling and touching. Ester hated having this man touch the photo. He held it for a long time and then handed it back. "I lied. I knew she was your granddaughter the moment I met you. You have the same eyes."

"And her mother and father?"

"They were handed over to the Uruguayan military."

"Do you know who has Mariana?"

"She is being raised by an officer and a gentleman. His wife is a devout Christian. The child will have the best education and upbringing."

Ester wanted to attack him, to hit and punch and kick him until he told her where Mariana was, but she pleaded with him instead, begged him to tell her where her granddaughter was. He would say no more about Mariana.

"It is time to move on, *señora*. To forget and look forward and not remain trapped in events."

Ester made herself sit with him until he finished his meal, making small talk in the hope that she could find a way to penetrate his defenses. No such opportunity presented itself.

She would have to be satisfied with what she had learned. Emi and Jorge had been alive when they were handed over to the Uruguayan military, and Mariana was somewhere in Argentina.

Ester went back to the newspaper and thanked the editor for what he had done.

"What will you do with the information?" he asked.

"I will go back to Montevideo and find the money to put ads in all the Buenos Aires papers."

She was sitting at the airport waiting to board when she saw the editor walking toward her. He pulled an envelope out of his pocket. "Everyone at the paper contributed something," he said.

"It should be enough to pay for the ads—big ones!"

For the first time since she had left on her journey, Ester burst into tears.

* * *

Twenty days after the quarter page ad appeared in the newspaper *Clarín* in Buenos Aires, the Mothers, whose number had been given in the ad, received a call reporting that a girl answering to Mariana's description was living in the home of Miguel Angel Furci, an agent, like the man Ester had interviewed in Brazil, of the *Secretaría de Información del Estado*—(State Information Service or SIDE). The Mothers investigated and learned that the birth certificate used to register the child had been obtained from the Civil Registry. The name given was Daniela Romina Furci, and the certificate noted that hers had been a home birth, on September 29, 1975. Convinced that the birth certificate was phony, the Mothers called Ester and asked if she would be willing to travel to Buenos Aires to see the child and make a positive identification.

One day later, Ester was sitting with Chicha Mariani in her office.

"The woman who saw this," Chicha said, pointing to the ad, "is sure that it's Mariana. We have a copy of the birth certificate, the phony one that the Furcis used to register her." She handed the copy to Ester.

"The date of birth is different, six months later than Mariana's."

"They did that all the time, to muddy the trail. See where it says that it was a home birth? That's another clue."

"What if I can't say for sure that it's her? Children change from one month to another, and it's been years since I saw her!"

"First, see the child. Then we'll decide what to do next."

The Mothers knew that the little girl walked to school every morning from her house one block away. Ester positioned herself where she could watch her pass by. Her heart was racing as she watched the child in her school uniform and braided hair making her way down the street. She feared that when the time came, she would be unable to move, but suddenly, she heard her singing.

"Mariana!"

The child was startled by Ester's sudden appearance. For a moment Ester thought she was going to run away. Then she raised her eyes and gave Ester the serious, quizzical look she had given her so many times and years before. They were Mariana's eyes, her unmistakable eyes.

* * *

"It was then that I buried my Emilia," she told Violeta the next day.

"Keep hoping, Ester."

Ester shook her head. "She's dead, Violeta. It's time to accept that."

"What are you going to do now that you've found Mariana?"

"I just wanted to grab her! Grab her and run!"

"Why didn't you?"

"A nine-year-old? It's not the same as a baby. She's had years with these people. She thinks they're her parents."

"What do the Mothers advise?"

"To apply to the courts to order the blood tests."

"That could take years!"

"What choice do I have? I have to think of her, of how to do this so that she's hurt as little as possible. When the blood tests prove who she is, then we'll find a way of breaking the news to her, of winning her back." Ester took a deep breath. "But what if she doesn't choose us, her family here? What will we do if she wants to stay with those people?"

"How could she, when she discovers that they killed her parents and kidnapped her?"

"And will we ever tell her that? How would we tell her?"

During the round of legal petitions requesting that the court order the blood tests proving Mariana's kinship to Ester, she kept herself busy finding out all she could about the Furcis, who she discovered were unable to produce any photos of Mariana before October of 1976. She prepared a room for Mariana in her house, filling it with books and photos of Emilia and Jorge and of Mariana herself as a baby.

The legal proceedings dragged on for a year and a half, passing through the hands of several judges, until finally the Furcis exhausted all of their appeals and the order was issued. The Furcis announced that they would allow their daughter Daniela to be tested, but they themselves would not give blood.

Their blood was unnecessary.

The tests proved Mariana's identity beyond the shadow of a doubt.

* * *

In April of 1984, Sara returned to Buenos Aires, where the process of gathering evidence against those who had instituted a reign of terror in Argentina was ongoing. The investigation had a two-fold purpose: to identify and bring to justice those accused of crimes against humanity; and to gather information about the disappeared from those who might have seen them before they vanished. Sara was asked to testify specifically about Automotores Orletti and what had happened there eight years before.

As part of the procedure surrounding the collection of evidence, witnesses were taken to the old garage. It was a somber gathering, and some witnesses came accompanied by a lawyer, a psychiatrist, or a physician.

Arriving at the site in daylight, this time with no hood to

impede her vision, Sara saw that Automotores Orletti was located in the midst of a residential area. The neighbors, she thought, must have gone about their business ignoring the screams, the comings and goings of cars and people.

She had no way of knowing how it had looked eight years ago, but in 1984 Automotores Orletti was a dilapidated, gloomy looking building, its sign rusted and hanging crookedly over the door. Entering the ground floor, she and the other witnesses found it packed with the belongings stolen from the disappeared, everything from motorcycles to shoes.

A man in a dark suit climbed the steps and turned to address them. "Good afternoon, my fellow citizens and visitors from Uruguay. I am Judge Victor Medina. Most of you have testified before me in recent years. We are nearing the end of this sad round of investigations and trials, and of our inadequate attempts to render justice. I say inadequate because the losses you have borne are beyond human justice. We are here at the request of survivors who asked if they could revisit this hell hole in an attempt to verify their memories of it. Many of you have your lawyers with you. We welcome them. Some of you have also brought your doctors and psychiatrists. We welcome them also. Roam where you will. If you see something belonging to you, please take it to the desk set up for claims. God be with you."

A few people moved over to look through the piles of belongings in case they recognized anything of their own among the booty, but most hung back. A few would have liked to find one or two prized possessions taken from their homes years before, and they approached the piles reluctantly, not wanting to rummage through objects that now seemed more like relics. The silence in the old garage was profound. Lawyers, judges, psychiatrists, and former prisoners stood together, each in their own way imagining or remembering what had happened in that building.

Sara's eyes were drawn to the steps leading up to the second floor. She recalled the many times she had ascended them, knowing as each day passed that it might be her last, and determined each time that she would go up as she had the first time. Where had she found the courage, she wondered? Or had it been rage?

The group shifted and moved, revealing a space under the steps where something glittered in the dim light. A man reached in and picked up the shining object. It was a jar full of wedding rings. He stood for a moment, stunned by the implication of what he had discovered, and then, as if he were raising a chalice, he held it up for the others to see. After they had looked at the jar and its sad, glittering contents for several long moments, it was handed to the judge and carried away to be examined for evidence.

A man pulled a blindfold from his pocket and was helped to tie it over his eyes. He was led to the stairs and began to climb, clearly knowing how many steps led to the top. There he stopped and turned to his left toward the truth chamber. Sara and several others followed him. Very little light filtered in from two small windows. Even though the equipment had been dismantled, the torture chamber retained its menace. Hooks pierced the walls and ceiling, and a chain lay in a corner. The man removed his blindfold and began touching the walls. Several others did the same, reaching out tentatively as if fearing that their touch might trigger a time warp and they would find themselves back in hell. No one chose to linger very long in the room, just long enough to add a visual dimension to blind recollections.

None of the witnesses present that day had ever been in the basement of the building, and they asked to see it now. Standing before a bullet-riddled wall still stained with blood, some cried for the first time, more affected by this mute testimony to the fate of many whose lives had ended there, than they had been by revisiting their own suffering.

The press was waiting for them when they left the building, as were many mothers and fathers of the disappeared, carrying photos of their children in the hope that those who had once been held at Orletti could provide news of them.

For the survivors, the simple acknowledgement that it was real, the courage to step back into the nightmare, and the Argentine Commission's desire to record the truth about what had happened there, marked the beginning of their recovery.

* * *

As a result of the publicity surrounding Sara's testimony, and in response to the ad the Mothers placed in the papers about Simón, a Mrs. Pelacoff telephoned the Mothers. She told them that she had worked with a young woman whose husband commanded a submarine fleet. The couple had two adopted children, a girl, and a red-headed boy, adopted in 1975 or 1976. A few weeks later, the Mothers received a second call confirming what they had heard from Mrs. Pelacoff. A Mr. Induraín reported that his wife had gone to school with a woman who had later adopted a red-headed baby found at the door of the church of San Isidro. The woman's husband, Mr. Induraín said, had worked at the submarine base in Mar del Plata, and was currently posted in Germany. He promised to look into the matter further, and not long afterwards provided a photo of the boy dressed as a marine and saluting for the camera.

Once more Sara traveled to Buenos Aires, to look at the photo and to request an interview with Mrs. Pelacoff. Gazing at the picture of the boy in his marine uniform, wanting desperately to recognize something about him, Sara had to admit that she had no idea if it was Simón. There might be a vague resemblance to Mauricio, but she was far from certain of it. Her hopes for a meeting with Mrs. Pelacoff were much higher, perhaps some essential detail would be remembered that would reveal whether or not this boy was really her son.

The Mothers arranged the meeting, and Sara was invited to visit Mrs. Pelacoff at her apartment. A uniformed maid answered the door and ushered her into a comfortable room, where Mrs. Pelacoff, in her mid-fifties, was waiting to receive her.

"I am so sorry about your grandson," Mrs. Pelacoff said, as she poured Sara a cup of tea.

"Simón is my son," Sara said.

"What? Your son?"

"Yes. I'm sorry if you were misinformed."

"But this is terrible!" Mrs. Pelacoff cried. "Terrible!"

Sara agreed that it was, but she felt there was more to Mrs. Pelacoff's distress than sympathy for a mother's loss. "I've been looking for him for almost eight years."

"Eight years! And you'll never stop, will you?"

"Never!"

"This is terrible!" Mrs. Pelacoff repeated. "I had hoped . . . you see . . . I thought I might be able to persuade a grandmother to stop searching once she knew the boy was with an excellent family, but a mother . . ."

Sara thought of Violeta and Ester, and of all the other grandmothers she had met who had not only never given up the search for their children and grandchildren; but had disappeared themselves as a result of having come too close to the truth of what had happened to them. This woman clearly lived in a very different world from Sara's, a world where it had been possible to remain both ignorant about and shielded from what was happening.

"Can you tell me what you know about the date when this boy was adopted?"

Mrs. Pelacoff told the story of how she and the boy's adoptive mother had worked together years before. The woman came from a military family, all the men had been in the armed forces, and she herself had married a navy officer. The dates of Simón's disappearance and the adoption of the boy coincided, and before long both of them were convinced that they were talking about Simón. Mrs. Pelacoff began to cry. "What will it mean to him to be taken from the only family he has ever known?"

Sara had been asking herself the same question, and soon she was also in tears. "He's living a lie, a deceit!" she said. She felt torn between feeling that Simón had a right to know his real parents, and the knowledge that this would only bring him pain.

* * *

Unable to do anything further until the submarine commander and his family returned from their post in Germany, Sara went back to Montevideo and wrote to Mauricio, informing him of her meeting with Mrs. Pelacoff. She was surprised to receive a call from him a few days later.

"I'm coming back," he said. "It's time."

Sara had a strange hollowness in the pit of her stomach when she hung up the phone. She would welcome Mauricio's support and his help with the search, but his return would dredge up old and unwelcome feelings. She recognized that Mauricio had a right to participate in the search for his son, but the lingering resentment at his long absence surfaced now that she knew he was coming back. They had talked about his departure, about how there was nothing he could have done to save her, of how he had believed that Simón was with her, or with a neighbor, of how his friends had persuaded him that he would be far more effective from abroad than as a fugitive in Argentina. Common sense battled with old notions of heroism and self-sacrifice. At the bottom of it all was a feeling that she and Simón might have been used as bait to trap Mauricio, and if so, he should have turned himself in. That this was sentimental nonsense, Sara knew. Even if he had turned himself in, they would not have released her, or told them where Simón was.

What would she have done if the tables had been turned? It was not a test she had been called upon to pass or fail, so she needed to put such thoughts behind her and focus on the future. Not only would she have to share Simón with Mauricio and deal with her resentment, but she would have to tell him to abandon all hope that the two of them would ever be a couple again. She had told him so before, but he had refused to accept it. Now there was Raúl to consider. They had resumed the friendship begun when they taught together—before Sara left to seek refuge in Buenos Aires—and as they got to know each other better, her respect for the work he was doing now to find the disappeared and to write about them, grew. They were in a deeply committed relationship and would soon be moving in together.

As the day of Mauricio's arrival approached, Raúl offered to go with her to the airport, but Sara knew that that would only make things more difficult. She met Mauricio's flight and waited in the arrival's lounge, watching as the passengers approached customs to pick up their luggage. Nearly an hour later the area had cleared and there was still no sign of Mauricio. Had he suffered another heart attack and been unable to travel? Sara was walking toward the Iberia Air Lines counter to ask if he had been aboard the flight, when she heard her name over the loudspeaker system, requesting that she report to the information desk. As she approached it, she saw him. He was looking the other way, so she had a moment to duck behind a sign and compose herself. He had aged twenty, not ten, years and looked deathly ill. His red hair had thinned and faded, and he moved as if he was carrying a heavy burden. She realized that he must have picked up his luggage without her recognizing him.

She put a smile on her face and went toward him, her resentment momentarily forgotten.

* * *

"Everything matches," Sara told him, "the dates, how he was found."

They were riding together in the back of a taxi, Mauricio looking out at sights at once familiar and profoundly altered during his long absence.

"Where was he?"

"On the steps of a church near our house."

"It was freezing that night."

"I remember."

Mauricio lit a cigarette.

"You shouldn't smoke. Your heart."

"It was my fault. We should have left in time."

"I didn't want to go either; to leave without knowing what had happened to Emi and the others."

"What are we going to do?"

"While we wait for the couple who has Simón to come back from Germany we'll start legal proceedings. Request a blood test. We're considered rather special, you and I."

Mauricio reached for her hand. "I've always known that."

Sara withdrew her hand gently from his. "We're the only surviving parents of a missing child."

"All the more reason for us to—."

"I'm seeing someone else, Mauricio."

The taxi stopped and before they could say anything more Mauricio's mother had run outside and was pulling the car door open. Weeping with joy, she took Mauricio in her arms and clung to him until he led her inside. Sara paid the driver and followed them. His aunts, uncles, and cousins were all waiting, and Sara and Mauricio weren't able to resume their conversation until the following day, when he asked if he could join her on her walk along the river.

"So who is this someone else?" he asked.

"His name is Raúl Olivera. I knew him before, from my teaching days."

"What are you doing now?"

"I've been offered a subsidy by the United Nations High Commission for Refugees to work with the Mothers. I'll be traveling back and forth between here and Buenos Aires. We're trying to locate all the Uruguayan children who disappeared. That's what I do now, try to find them all."

"How many were there?"

"Seventeen that we know of."

"One of them little Mariana," he sighed. "How did we get to this place, Sara? How did we go from wanting to make the world better to living in a nightmare?"

"I spent five years in prison asking myself that question and I—"

"No need to throw that in my face on my second day back!" He grabbed her arm and spun her toward him. "I want to start over. I've changed. Really changed. I was a fool. Always taking things for granted, thinking I was invincible. Gerardo died. You went to prison. Simón disappeared. A man doesn't live through things like that and stay the same."

"I don't blame you for saving yourself. There was nothing you could have done."

"You blame me for Simón. If I had looked that night—"

"You thought he was with me."

"I didn't look!"

"So what do you want from me?" Sara shouted, the wind catching at her words. "Absolution?"

"Understanding, Sara! A little mercy! You were always so sure of yourself. So confident. You never put a foot wrong. I've heard about you at Orletti, how they couldn't break you. How self-righteous you must feel! Sara the strong. Sara the heroic.

While her husband ran off to Spain with his tail between his legs!"

"You were never my husband!"

"And you resent that as well? That I never married you?"

"I thought you said you'd changed? Can't you see that none of it had anything to do with you? It wasn't you or me I was thinking of at Orletti! It wasn't for you that I spent months in solitary. It was for Simón! The only reason I didn't die was Simón! The only reason I live is Simón!"

"And Raúl?"

"Yes. And Raúl."

* * *

Sara's work with the Mothers was challenging. Often those who had reported the birth or disappearance of a missing child had left the country; and locating them abroad was difficult. The authorities that might have provided key information were not only uncooperative, but often they defended the perpetrators, claiming they had been doing their duty defending their countries from terrorists and insurgents. Families of the disappeared were still fearful that if they "made waves" with their inquiries, the missing relative, who they hoped was still alive, might be tortured or killed in retribution.

While nothing further surfaced about Simón, other families published photos and information in the Buenos Aires newspapers. Among the photos was Amaral's—the first Uruguayan child to disappear—along with his parents, Yolanda and Floreal. A month after their disappearance Yolanda and Floreal's bodies were found, but there was no sign of three-year-old Amaral. Knowing how much Amaral's family had already been through, Sara proceeded very cautiously when a midwife called Isabel Pereyra telephoned the Mother's headquarters to report that nine years ago a woman had asked her to issue a birth certificate for a little boy whose mother, the woman had said, abused him dreadfully and only wanted money for him. He had been offered to the woman's daughter, Dorothy, who was desperate for a child and would gladly pay the price the boy's mother was asking. Thinking she could only do good by removing a child from an abusive situation, the midwife issued the false birth certificate and only wondered about it years later when she learned that Dorothy and her husband worked for the secret service. Among the many cases of desperate biological and adoptive mothers she had dealt with, this one had stuck in her memory for another reason, the child's unusual name—Amaral.

Sara enlisted Isabel Pereyra's help in tracking down Dorothy's family, and impressed upon her the importance of proceeding with the utmost care. The midwife performed her task diligently, and was able to discover that Amaral's adoptive parents, as well as Dorothy, the grandmother who had requested the birth certificate, had died, and that Amaral, now known as Juan Manuel, lived with a grandfather. This grandfather was critically ill and hospitalized, so the boy was staying with a neighbor.

Only then did Sara notify Amaral's aunt and uncle, Maricel and Alberto, who traveled to Buenos Aires at once. Sara filled them in about everything she had learned, and they decided that Alberto would stroll by the place where Amaral played with his friends and pretend to ask for directions. Apart from his unusual name, Amaral had a strong, prominent nose to distinguish him, and Alberto was quite certain he would recognize his nephew.

As soon as the group of boys came out to play, Alberto walked by and engaged them in casual conversation. There was the unmistakable nose! Alberto asked their names. Amaral answered simply that he didn't really know, he had had several. Alberto almost lost his composure when he heard this reply. It took all his willpower not to snatch up his nephew and take him then and there.

Alberto soon wished that he had done exactly that, because a week after being identified, Amaral disappeared again. This time it did not take years but days to discover where he was. His elder "brother" Quico had taken him to Formosa where he worked for the secret services of the Armed Forces. Maricel and Alberto instigated the legal proceedings necessary to begin the blood tests that would prove their relationship to Amaral; and Quico threatened to flee. Once more, the temptation to circumvent legalities and take the boy was overwhelming, and again it was resisted.

Maricel and Alberto's patience and determination paid off, and they were able to claim their nephew with a duly processed court order. Amaral was the first Uruguayan child to disappear and the first to be found. He stated that he wanted to be told everything about his history.

Sara and the Mothers celebrated with a party at Chicha Mariani's house. Aunt Maricel, Uncle Alberto and Amaral walked in to find a table laden with traditional Uruguayan dishes. *Pascualina* (spinach pie), homemade *ñoquis* (Italian gnocci) with meat and tomato sauces, *dulce de leche* (similar to caramelized condensed milk), ice cream, and in the back garden, meats roasting on a grill.

Amaral had grown into a tall pre-teen and was remarkably composed. He kissed and was kissed by everyone present and laughed when asked how it felt to have a new name. "I have always wanted to know who I really am," he said, making for the food table. His aunt and uncle watched as he heaped his plate with food and they whispered to Chicha to please excuse his manners.

Amaral cleared his plate and as he walked to the table for a second helping asked if this is what he could expect from the relatives waiting in Montevideo.

"This and more!" said Chicha. "I've heard there's a bicycle awaiting you!"

"And a soccer ball," Sara added.

"And schoolbooks . . ." said his aunt Maricel.

Amaral grinned. "I like school, *tía!*"

Chicha put her arm around Sara. "One day soon we will be doing this for you and Simón."

* * *

While Sara was waiting for the couple whom she believed had Simón to return from overseas duty, another lead surfaced, and she and Mauricio pursued it. A red-headed baby had been adopted by a single woman in the Province of Corrientes, and those who had been watching the boy assured Sara that he even walked like her. Sara and Mauricio followed the woman and child onto a train and observed the boy, Mauricio from behind a pair of dark glasses, Sara from behind her newspaper. The red curly hair was there, along with freckles, and a wide forehead. Sara thought of all the red-headed children she had watched over the years who shared these same characteristics. When her search began, she thought that surely when she saw Simón she would know him from all others. What kind of parents would they be, she and Mauricio asked themselves, if they didn't feel something special when they saw their own son?

Like the leads before, this one also turned out to be false, and the waiting and the searching resumed.

They had no previous cases to resort to for help in understanding and dealing with the complexity of the situation and the feelings they were experiencing. Guilt overwhelmed them both, particularly Mauricio. He kept returning to the theme of not having left in time, confessing to having been afraid of being thought a coward if he opted for exile while so many others were staying behind to fight. As Sara had feared, he would not give up on the idea of resuming their relationship—the two of them against the world—and they quarreled incessantly.

"You've never done anything to find him! He's my son! I was the one who wanted to have him! You never claimed him!"

"Because I didn't know if the *milicos*[*] knew about us! I wanted to protect you!"

"Liar! You knew they knew!"

They tried therapy. The therapist told Sara that she had to learn to live with her losses.

"I can't," Sara said. "Nor do I want to."

As other children were identified and Sara watched families trying to absorb and understand the magnitude of what had happened to them, she took to examining her own feelings more and more.

From the Mothers point of view, Simón had been taken as war booty and rightfully belonged to his mother. Sara on the other hand, feared that he might reproach her, for everything. From the choices she had made that had endangered their lives, to the choice of revealing his real identity. Does everyone have the right to know the truth about themselves? Or would it be best to leave Simón where he was, even if his existence was a lie and a travesty? Surely her duty as a mother was to spare her son any suffering she could. Even if it meant abandoning her role as a mother, she should do it to spare him the anguish of an identity crisis. Not only would she be revealing to him that he was adopted, but that those whom he had thought of as his parents until now, had in all likelihood played a part in Sara's kidnapping. Was his right to know these things worth the grief that would follow? What if he was restored to her and his values were different from her own? They might not love or even like each other.

After their first emotional meeting, Mrs. Pelacoff had refused to see Sara again, but the other informant, Mr. Induraín, continued to provide data to the Mothers. He reported that the family

---

[*] A derogatory term for the military.

who he believed had Simón were due back soon, at which time he would be paying them a visit. He undertook to question the couple and to provide proof of whatever they told him. They would have news before Christmas.

Every day, Sara sat by the phone, thinking each time it rang that this might be the call she was waiting for. One morning, she was in Buenos Aires working at her desk at the Mother's headquarters when Chicha approached her.

One look at her face confirmed that she did not have good news. "Tell me," Sara said.

"I'm so sorry, Sara," Chicha said, putting a copy of a certificate of adoption on the desk. "He was adopted in April of 1976, three months before Simón was born."

* * *

For Ester, obtaining permission to remove Mariana from the Furci's custody proved to be as slow and difficult as the previous proceedings relating to the blood tests. Ester gave interviews to the press and appeared on television, but nothing seemed to motivate the courts to act.

Early in 1985, a telegram signed by Mariana, under her new name, reached Ester. It read: "I will never forget the harm you are doing to my family. My parents love me and I love them. Daniela Romina Furci."

A day later a typewritten letter* arrived, dated Buenos Aires, January 21, 1985. Mariana was nine years old at the time.

Madam,

> *About 48 hours ago I sent a telegram to your home in the Republic of Uruguay and I did so due to the indignation produced in me by your assertions regarding my family. Indignation is not*

---

* Translated by the author, maintaining the punctuation and syntax of the original.

all that I feel, I also feel disgust, hatred and all that, you know; it's wrong of me to say these things because as a Christian I learned among other things that: "You will love the Lord your God with all your heart, with all your soul, with all your mind" – this is the greatest and first commandment and the second (in case you don't know) is: "You will love your neighbor like yourself." Of course you know nothing of such things, you would never accept "Giving Caeser what is Caeser's and God what is God's". You obviously blindly obey and give loyalty to other authorities. Our religion, madam, teaches that the divine authority of a Supreme Being is above all other authority, that's why you and many others are dedicated to the destruction of religion. I think you are an atheist... I don't know, but I think so.

In my home—the one you cynically claim I don't belong to—religious principles are taught and you will never succeed in neutralizing this paternal influence. For Argentines, and for all Catholics, "religion is not the opium of the people," on the contrary, it comforts us, gives us strength to fight against people like you.

As you know—for you made these statements in the newspaper La Razón—I attend a private religious school, the Holy Child Virgin Mary School. I attend catechism classes which fill me with joy. I forgot to tell you that the "person" you say you "saw" is my mother, Elena María González de Furci, so be more respectful, don't be so presumptuous as to treat her so disparagingly as a certain "person."

How much hatred you must feel for me and for my family, of course my parents teach me the best of things and educate me like the good Christians they are. They can't imagine me accepting the teachings and doctrines of some Party, like you must have taught your children to do. I say this as a simple deduction . . . otherwise explain to me what your daughter and son-in-law were doing in my country instead of being in Uruguay in the bosom of their family, who were they? Guerrillas?... I ask because I don't know.

The letter went on in this vein for two more pages, and closed with an apocalyptic quote:

Then came one of the seven angels who had the seven cups, and he spoke with me, and he said: Come and I shall show you the judgment of a prostitute who is seated on the great waters, with whom the kings of the earth have fornicated, and earth's dwellers have become drunk with the wine of her fornication. A spirit took me to the desert, and I saw a woman seated on a red beast, her name was blasphemy, she had seven heads and ten horns.

It was signed, *Daniela Furci*, and was followed two days later by another letter extolling the values of the family and religion. It was obvious that a nine-year-old child had not written them. Their ranting, "demented" nature filled Ester and all of Mariana's family with concern over the education she was receiving and the person she would become under the Furci's influence. They consulted a psychologist for advice on how best to proceed, what steps to take in order to hurt Mariana as little as possible. The psychologist advised caution, a gentle and gradual introduction to the subject of her biological parents, with as little mention of the Furcis as possible.

And then Mariana disappeared for the second time. In June of 1985 Furci reported that his wife had taken the child and left. A few days later, he too, was gone.

When Ester heard the news, she felt her knees buckle. Violeta caught her and eased her onto the sofa.

"I've never fainted in my life," Ester said, "let me up!"

"In a minute! You're as white as a sheet!"

"I'm going to Buenos Aires!"

She left that day and oversaw the issuance of orders for the Furcis' arrest and the printing and dissemination of posters with their photos.

* * *

Sara and Ester were among the thousands who protested the amnesty granted to the Uruguayan military. Simón, if he was alive, would be ten years old; Mariana, eleven. Holding their pictures high, they marched, demanding a referendum on the issue. They also joined the group Mothers and Relatives of the Detained-Disappeared and created a National Pro-Referendum Commission.

Uruguay's constitution requires that 25 percent of voters sign a petition requesting a referendum before an issue can be voted upon. People were painfully aware that during the years of the dictatorship, signatures from other petitions, dating as far back as 1950, had been unearthed and people had been questioned about them.

In spite of this history, Ester was convinced that the courage to sign would be found, and she agreed to serve as President of the Commission.

Meanwhile, the Mothers and Relatives of the Detained-Disappeared initiated a civil suit against the joint military and police forces. Major Gavazzo was summoned to testify but did not respond to the summons. A second summons was issued, with the judge reminding the Major that he could be compelled to appear. The Minister of Defense then announced that both citations were in a safe and no military officer would appear before a judge in a civil court. On December 22, 1986, one hour before the judge's order would have been enforced and Gavazzo, now a Colonel, compelled to appear in court, a new amnesty law was passed. Under its provisions, military and police personnel could not be prosecuted even in a civil court for human rights violations occurring between 1973 and 1985. Thirty-eight pending cases were dismissed.

In Argentina, events were taking a very different course. President Raúl Alfonsín had been in power for two years, and investigations into the atrocities committed during the military dictatorship were ongoing, with the names of those responsible being made public. Nine commanders were brought before a civil court and charged with murder, torture, and abduction. Defense lawyers argued that the commanders had not personally participated in any of the crimes for which they stood accused, and that the crimes had been committed as excesses by certain individuals. The court was not swayed, and ruled that the commanders would be held responsible for the actions of their subordinates.

The entire effort was condemned by the Uruguayan military as part of an international Communist conspiracy orchestrated from Moscow and New York.

In April of 1986, Argentina's National Commission on the Disappeared formally requested the extradition of three members of Uruguay's military forces, Colonel Nino Gavazzo among them. The Uruguayan chancellery did not respond, and the three men were tried and found guilty *in absentia.*

CHAPTER VIII

The 1984 United Nations Convention against Torture and Other Cruel, Inhuman, and Degrading Treatment or Punishment describes torture as "any act by which severe pain or suffering, whether physical or mental, is intentionally inflicted by or at the instigation of a public official on a person for such purposes as obtaining information. No exceptional circumstances whatsoever, whether a state of war or a threat of war, internal political instability, or any other public emergency may be invoked as a justification for torture."

Having a child together was a gift beyond anything Sara and Raúl had hoped for, but at age forty-three Sara, to their great joy, became pregnant. Unlike others whose heart and lungs had been damaged by prolonged torture, starvation, and infection, Sara's vital organs had not been affected by her ten days at Orletti. She had regained almost complete mobility in her arms and hands, and the aches and pains that sometimes assailed her were not serious enough to cause deep concern. She felt healthier than ever, and flourished during her pregnancy.

Mauricio had at last accepted that there was no hope of resuming their relationship. He had returned to his ceramics work, although friends told Sara that he was drinking heavily and at night often destroyed the pieces he had created during the day. Their search for Simón kept them in close communication. Sara knew that Mauricio's mother, unable to accept her son Gerardo's disappearance, often questioned Mauricio about why more had not been done to save his brother.

Sara was seven months pregnant when she visited Mauricio in his workshop to deliver the latest information about Simón. He opened the door and stood back to look at her. "Seeing you like that takes me back a few years." He stepped aside. "Come in."

"The workshop looks wonderful."

"You were never a good liar. What's up? You're nervous."

"I found out that a couple of weeks after Simón disappeared, a friend of Gavazzo's showed up with a baby. The boy's hair isn't red, it's more chestnut—"

"It could have got darker in eleven years."

"They named him Gerardo."

"Wouldn't that be a strange coincidence?" Mauricio smiled sadly, remembering his brother. "What do you know about the adoption?"

"Nothing. The woman claims to have given birth to him, but I discovered that she had two miscarriages before Gerardo and that she and her husband were on several adoption lists."

"We should arrange a meeting with them."

There was a knock at the door.

"That's Raúl," Sara said. "We're on our way to the doctor and we're late."

Mauricio opened the door.

"I'm coming!" Sara called.

"Come in, *hombre,*" Mauricio said. "There's no reason for you to stand out there on the curb."

Raúl held out his hand and Mauricio took it, pulling Raúl into a hug. "Watch out for her!" he said, as they were leaving. "Last time she was in labor she nearly had the baby in the car."

"I'm having so many checkups this one will be born with a stethoscope instead of ears!"

"Sara, you made a joke," Mauricio laughed.

"She makes jokes all the time," Raúl said.

"You must be good for her."

* * *

Two hours later Sara was sitting on the beach looking at the river, her arms wrapped tightly around her knees. Raúl was caressing her hair.

"The doctor says the chances are fifty-fifty. They can operate right after you deliver!"

Sara looked at her hands. "How big do you think a baby's lungs are?"

"They perform miracles these days."

The baby, they had discovered, had a malformation of the diaphragm that had prevented the healthy development of one of the pulmonary lobes. An operation could be performed, but Sara needed to prepare herself for the fact that the baby might not survive. She wanted to know if it was her fault. Was the defect a result of the electric shocks, or of the beatings? The doctors assured her that they had no reason to think so, but for several days Sara could focus on nothing else. Finding Simón took on fresh urgency. If the baby lived, Sara's time would be absorbed in nursing her, but if she died . . . Only by focusing all her energy on the latest in a series of reports about Simón could she keep her terror at bay. Hard work had come to her aid on more than one occasion, and it did not fail her now. Hoping that Gerardo's parents would consent to a blood test, Sara and Mauricio appealed for help from Mr. Rosella, the director of the boy's school. Would he, as an impartial third party, arrange a meeting at which Mauricio and Sara could tell their story to the couple? Rosella did not hesitate, and in early September of 1987, the meeting took place.

Rosella did his best to let Gerardo's parents know how much he appreciated their willingness to meet with Sara and Mauricio, and appealed to their compassion for an eleven-year search for a son. Sara told the story of her arrest and of how she had left Simón. Mauricio went over everything he had researched about the day Simón disappeared and also revealed what he now knew about young Gerardo—that he had not been born to Zully Morales as she first claimed, but found in a garbage can when he was two months old, bearing a sign that read "My name is Marcelo Alejandro. Whoever takes me, give me lots of love."

That child, Zully and her husband Carlos said, was undernourished and weak, unlike the baby Sara had just described as her own.

"All the formalities were observed," Carlos said.

"We applied for custody of Marcelo Alejandro and carried out all the legal procedures to complete the adoption."

"May we see the papers?" Mauricio asked.

Zully and Carlos became agitated. "The papers have been lost," Carlos said.

"But we don't need the papers to know that Gerardo is ours!" Zully said, bursting into tears. "What you've said proves nothing! Nothing."

"Please," Sara pleaded, "we understand how painful this is for you. We don't want to make what we've all gone through any worse. It can all be resolved so easily with a blood test."

"We guarantee absolute privacy for you and for your family," Mauricio assured them.

"Gerardo doesn't even need to know that it's anything more than a routine blood test for school," Rosella said.

"We don't want to upset him or you," Sara added.

"You've upset us already!" Carlos said. "Your search for your son has been written up in all the papers. Every time you think you've found him, or one of the others, everybody gets hounded by the press! Every child in Uruguay born since 1972 thinks he's a child of the disappeared!"

"Only *you* haven't disappeared!" Zully said.

"Don't you think that Gerardo has a right to know who he is?"

"He knows he's adopted. And all he wants is to live in peace with us. We are his parents!"

"We know that you love him," Sara said. "That he loves you. Even if the test were to prove that he's our son, we wouldn't do anything until we had worked it out together."

"You think that's a risk we're going to take?" Carlos asked. "A blood test is out of the question."

"Then you leave us no choice," Mauricio said. "We'll see you in court."

Carlos stood up. "To hell with your courts! Let's go, Zully!"

"How can you be so selfish?" Zully asked. "You're having another baby! Gerardo is all I have!"

The meeting was a failure, and from the moment they parted, Sara wished she could start over again, that she could find the words with which to reassure Carlos and Zully that they were not adversaries, that she was as frightened of the truth as they were; and would do everything in her power to ensure a happy outcome, especially for the boy.

* * *

Sara was in bed, trying to rest after a sleepless night, when the telephone rang. It was Ester.

"I'm calling to say goodbye!"

"Where are you going now?" Sara asked.

"We've heard that the Furcis might be in Paraguay. Violeta and I are leaving in a few hours!"

"Where in Paraguay? Do you have any idea? You can't search the whole country!"

"Oh, can't I?"

Sara laughed. "Well, yes, if anyone can, you can!"

"They're supposed to be in Asunción, so I won't have to go into the jungle if that's what you're worrying about."

A few days later they were back.

"We combed Asunción," she told Sara, "north to south, east to west. Down alleys, avenues, and dirt roads."

They'd been told that the Furcis were running a food store, so they visited every one they came across. "We worked all day, except at noon, when it was so hot we couldn't move! But afterwards we kept going until late at night. I went to every Catholic school in the phone book. Nothing."

"I'm so sorry, Ester," Sara said.

"On the way back we stopped in Buenos Aires and I went to see Mariana's 'grandmother'—that woman's mother!"

"Did she talk to you?"

"Oh, yes! She's in worse shape than I am! She took me into the room where Mariana used to sleep when she stayed with her and she cried every second I was there! She doesn't know where they are either and I ended up feeling sorry for her. You should have seen the room! There were about twenty dolls on the bed, all in different outfits. Not a single book, not one photograph! What must Mariana's mind be filled with?"

* * *

The doctors determined that Sara should remain under close medical observation during the last month of her pregnancy, and she entered the hospital for complete bed rest.

Raúl sat by her every evening until late at night, reading to her, watching television with her, bringing her newspapers, magazines and books, and complaining that he couldn't keep up with the pace of her reading. One member or another of her family came every day to see her, and Ester kept Sara informed about what was happening with the committees on which they both served.

One night, when she and Raúl were alone, he stopped reading in the middle of a sentence. Sara looked at him expectantly. He smiled. "I was just seeing if you were paying attention. I've been doing a lot of thinking. We should get married."

"Why now?"

"Because I love you profoundly. Because we are having a child. Because I want to be able to say the words 'my wife.' I would be so proud if you would have me."

A few days later, on the 9th of November 1987, Sara left her room briefly for a quick ceremony at a nearby courthouse. Her entire family and Raúl's, plus Violeta, Ester, Blanca, and several friends were there to witness the marriage, and when she and Raúl had signed the register as husband and wife, they all went back to the hospital where the nurses joined them for cake and champagne, taking it in turns to toast them in the small, crowded room.

Two days later, Sara gave birth to a daughter. They named her María Emilia. Handing her over to the surgeons was the most difficult thing Sara had ever done. She didn't want to be parted from her for a single instant, and wondered, in fact, if she would ever be able to allow her child to leave her sight. A nurse took her gently from Sara and she watched as they disappeared down the long corridor.

Two hours later, when the surgeon entered her room, Sara knew before he spoke that her baby had not survived the operation.

* * *

Sara and Raúl buried their daughter and their grief. She would be remembered in the commitment they made to devote the rest of their lives to finding Simón and the other disappeared children.

On the day before the Feast of the Holy Innocents, December 27, 1987, a church service was held commemorating those children, and Sara and Raúl, accompanied by Mary's mother, Blanca, attended the service. It was interrupted for Blanca by a neighbor who slipped in beside her to say that there was a man at her house with papers for Blanca to sign. "He has news of your granddaughter!"

Blanca crossed herself hastily and arrived at her house breathless, accompanied by Sara and Raúl. Veronica had been found, living with a relative of Oscar Penna's, just as they had suspected.

The next day, Blanca and her husband were in Buenos Aires with Chicha Mariani at the Mothers' headquarters. They were introduced to a doctor who Blanca thought had the kindest eyes of anyone she had ever met. He kissed her cheek and Blanca hugged him. Her hand in his, she sat and listened to what Chicha had to tell her.

"A teacher, who knew that one of the little girls in her class was adopted, saw our television program about disappeared children—the one where you spoke about Mary—and she came to us. The little girl is living with Oscar Penna's sister."

"It's her!"

"We think so. Penna's sister was married to the man who was taken to see Mary while she was at Banfield. Are you ready to take the blood tests?"

"Take all my blood if it helps to prove who she is!"

The doctor laughed. "Thankfully, that won't be necessary! One little vial will do nicely!"

The doctor always went in person to obtain the test results, and while they were being processed, Blanca and her husband met with a judge to discuss the legal proceedings that would follow if the tests proved positive, and with the psychologist who explained to them that she would be the one breaking the news to Veronica.

Depending on her reaction, they would decide what to do next. Blanca and her husband were to prepare themselves for rejection. Veronica was nine years old, a difficult age for many girls. She had been living with María Elena Maurino and her husband, now deceased, all her life, and even if she had been told she was adopted, it was likely that she was extremely attached to her adoptive parents, especially her mother. She also did not know that the name her parents had given her was María Victoria.

"You'll know right away what the results are," Chicha told them when they met again two days later.

"The doctor does have very expressive eyes," Blanca agreed.

"Oh, you'll know before you can even read his eyes! You'll see!"

They sat by the window and waited for him to come, watching as other pedestrians walked by. All of a sudden, Chicha smiled. "Look!" she said.

The doctor had just turned the corner. He was carrying half a dozen bottles of cider and a large box of what could only be *masitas*, the little pastries Blanca loved.

It was December 30th, 1987, the tenth anniversary of Mary and Fredi's disappearance, and their daughter had regained her true identity. She was being transferred to a foster home even as they spoke; and was in the company of the psychiatrist who had spoken to Blanca and her husband. A court appointment had been set for the following day, New Year's Eve.

When Blanca and her husband arrived, they were invited into a patio at the courthouse, a shady, tiled retreat, with a small fountain surrounded by plants and flowers. A table had been laid with a white tablecloth, and bottles of cider, champagne, finger sandwiches, *pan dulce*, and cake. Veronica was already in the building with her foster mother, and the psychiatrist was explaining everything to her. Just before the judge escorted her in, the psychiatrist told Blanca and her husband that the issue of her name had not been discussed, so for the time being it would be best to address her as Veronica.

When she saw her granddaughter walking in on the judge's arm, Blanca felt transported back thirty years. It was Mary at age ten who was coming toward her. There was the same dark, shoulder length curly hair, the curious, bright brown eyes, the smile.

She and her husband sat frozen, not knowing how to react when the judge introduced them. Veronica seemed completely at her ease. She kissed them, sat at the table as if she had known them all her life, and helped pass round the sandwiches. She was avid for information about her parents, her grandparents, her cousins, aunts and uncles. Any awkwardness there might have been was soon dispelled in the rush of her questions, and Blanca and her husband took it in turns to tell family stories, avoiding all reference to what had happened to Veronica's parents.

"They told me I had no relatives," Veronica said simply.

"The people who had you told you this?" Blanca asked her.

"The woman who had me. Her husband died when I was about a year old. I don't remember him at all."

"So you knew . . .?" Blanca hesitated, looking at the psychiatrist.

"I knew that I was adopted," Veronica said. "They told me that my mother was dead and that my father had given me away."

Her grandfather gasped and spilled cider down the front of his shirt. "He would have loved you with a passion, but he was killed months before you were born."

Veronica looked about to cry and the psychiatrist stepped in. "I think you have some photos to show Veronica?" she said.

"Yes, yes!" Blanca said eagerly, reaching for her handbag and spreading the photos of Fredi and Mary on the table.

Veronica picked up the photos one by one, caressing her dead parents' faces. Until that moment the enormity of what was happening to her had not sunk in, but as she looked at the image of Mary and saw herself, she seemed to age, until every gesture reminded Blanca of her daughter. They all sat silent, trying not to stare, realizing that Veronica had retreated into a world of her own, oblivious to their presence.

Blanca was not a superstitious woman, but she felt that Mary was communicating with her daughter, and that Veronica was silently telling her all the things she had longed to say to her mother during the last nine years.

* * *

In Uruguay, plans were going ahead for a referendum on whether or not to revoke the amnesty granted to the military for crimes committed during the dictatorship. Ester's belief that her countrymen and women would find the courage to sign the petition requesting a referendum proved accurate. The law required 525,000 signatures. 595,000 people put their names to the petition.

The recount and verification of signatures took a year. Any name that appeared to have been altered or corrected was discounted. By invalidating signatures where there was the slightest discrepancy, the electoral commission managed to bring the number below the required level. In violation of their right to confidentiality, the names and addresses of those whose signatures had come under scrutiny were published, and they were invited to re-sign during a three day period, at sites that remained open only during working hours. As it was revealed that the names of well-known union and political leaders were on the list, accusations flew.

In spite of all the difficulties, the number of ratifications necessary to call for a referendum was met. Ester and the Pro-Referendum Committee were elated. The campaign could now begin. They had two months to persuade voters to revoke the amnesty given to the military.

"The worst part," Ester complained to Sara, "is confronting the daily, intense, malicious propaganda put out by the government!"

"Have you heard the latest ad?" Sara asked her.

"How could I help it? Their trucks keep going by blaring it out over the loudspeakers!"

"The Tupamaros will vote green," it announced in reference to the color of the paper on which the referendum was printed. "The Communists vote green! How are *you* going to vote?"

Sara went on television in an ad supporting the referendum. Her calm, serious face looked at the viewers directly, and in a steady, gentle voice, she asked "Will you help me find my son?"

The voting took place on April 16, 1989.

The results from the capital were overwhelmingly in support of the revocation of the amnesty given to the military, but as results began to filter in from the rest of the country, Ester despaired. The revocation failed. She thought back on the months she had spent presenting example after example of how her countrymen and women had been physically and psychologically tortured, of how rare it was for a family not to have a friend, a relative, someone affected by the repressive methods employed over the previous decade and wondered what more she could have done.

"They don't understand what's at stake!" she said.

Sara and Violeta worried that this latest loss would permanently affect Ester's health. She had worked almost non-stop for a year, only to see the revocation initiative fail. "People need to be more conscious of their rights and duties," she raged to Sara. "Especially of their rights."

"Do you think there was fraud involved?"

"That would make it easier to accept the outcome," Ester sighed, her anger evaporating. "I think it was fear. For over ten years any action could be used against us. Who knows how long it will take before we can wipe out the effects of that on the nation's psyche."

The Mental Health and Human Rights Institute of Latin America agreed with Ester that the failure of the revocation vote was an indication of the poor health of the body social. "The community administered its own punishment: forgetting. But amnesty does not bring about amnesia."

Whether what happened next was a distraction or additional stress, Sara couldn't say. Probably both, she and Violeta concluded.

Furci, the man who had Mariana, telephoned Ester.

"They've left Paraguay and are back in Buenos Aires. He wants to meet," Ester said. "He must have realized that as long as I'm alive he'll never get a moment's peace."

"I'll come with you."

"He said I have to go alone."

"Ester—"

"What can he do to me that he hasn't already done?"

"Have him arrested!"

"Listen, Sara, I've been working through the courts for years and it's got me nowhere. My only hope is to be allowed to see Mariana, to persuade her to leave them. I can't take her away from them against her will, that would only make her situation worse. I won't wait for the courts anymore."

Ester traveled to Buenos Aires on the hydrofoil, eager at last to confront the man who had taken her granddaughter. As instructed, on arrival she sat in the waiting room. She had brought a book with her, but found herself re-reading every sentence, unable to absorb anything, rehearsing over and over in her mind what she would say to win Mariana back.

A man in mismatched jacket and trousers approached her and confirmed who she was.

"And you, is your name Furci?"

"No, *señora*. He is waiting outside."

They left the terminal and walked toward the parking lot, where a man in a dark suit was standing next to a small white car. He was of medium height and build, with dark hair and a nervous manner. His jacket was too snug to conceal the gun and holster strapped under it.

"You told me to come alone, but you brought a companion," Ester said.

"He's nobody," Furci said, opening the car door for her.

Ester turned to the man who had escorted her to the car. "Why do you let him refer to you as nobody?"

"I mean," Furci said, "that he's here to take care of you."

Ester laughed. "I don't need him. You're the one who's afraid." She looked at his coat as she got into the passenger seat. "You need a better tailor. The one who cut that coat doesn't know how to conceal a gun."

They proceeded to a café, where they all ordered coffee. Furci's companion took his and sat a few tables away.

"Where is Mariana?" Ester asked, coming straight to the point.

"Daniela isn't Mariana."

"Is that why I came to Buenos Aires? To hear more lies?"

"We've had the blood tests. Our blood is the same."

"If that were true, we wouldn't be talking. Let's face the facts. Sooner or later, you'll have to give her up or go to jail for abducting a minor."

"Don't you want to know about her? About our family?"

"I know everything I need to know. You wrote me a letter, remember?"

"Daniela wrote that letter."

"If she did it gives me all the more reason to want to remove her from your pernicious influence."

"What a fierce woman you are," he said, sitting back in his chair and studying her.

"My name is blasphemy, your letter said. I have seven heads and ten horns to be fierce with!"

For the briefest of moments a look of fear crossed Furci's face.

"I want to know about Mariana."

"She's a very happy young woman. She plays the piano, she loves to dance. She's pretty, like you, with light eyes."

"What have you told her?"

"Nothing. How would I tell her? What would I tell her?"

"Start by telling her she's adopted. That you chose her. She must know you love her."

"Children never know how much their parents love them until they become parents themselves."

"You're spouting cheap sentimentality at me? You and your cronies killed my only child. You stole my grandchild."

"Please! Let's not insult each other. We're in a very unique and difficult position."

"Yours will only get more difficult. You don't control the judges anymore."

"Are you threatening me?"

"This is getting very tiresome. We both know why I'm here. I want to see Mariana. I want her identity restored to her. You want to avoid going to jail."

"All I want is to avoid hurting my daughter."

"Then you should have given her to her family fourteen years ago."

"Do you mind if I smoke?"

"Go ahead."

He lit a cigarette, the match shaking. "It may take me a while to persuade my wife to allow you to see Daniela."

"I'll wait. For a week. No longer."

"I may need a little more time."

"Two weeks. Not a day more." Ester picked up her handbag and stood up.

Furci also stood, and to Ester's surprise, kissed her goodbye.

She submitted to being touched by him only because she wanted to do nothing more to antagonize him, but once she was in the car with the driver, she rubbed and rubbed at her cheek until it stung.

* * *

"Has he called yet?" Sara asked Ester three weeks later.

"He called," Ester replied, "and set up another meeting. I went to Buenos Aires and sat in the waiting room at the docks all day. I saw him once, looking in, but by the time I got outside he had disappeared. I waited until the last ship left. He never came. Jorge's family is going to take over for a while. I'm afraid that if I ever see that man again, I'll kill him!"

"You need to rest, Ester."

"No, Sara. I need to know what happened to Emi and Jorge. I need Mariana back."

"We'll do it, Ester. Things are changing."

"Too slowly!"

"Yes. But they are changing. You know the civil suit that those of us who were brought over from Orletti filed against the government?* The judge decided he wanted to visit some of the locales where prisoners were held by the military, and two days before his visit, the Minister of Defense made us an offer. $250,000 for each of us."

Ester gasped. "A fortune, Sara!"

"More money than I thought I'd ever see!"

"What are you going to do with it?"

"Buy a house. Help my family. Help everyone who's looking for their children."

"And the business with Zully and Carlos Morales and their son?"

Sara sighed and threw up her hands. "A mess! We were finally

---

* Unable to prosecute the military, Sara and others brought charges against the government itself.

able to get a court order to have Gerardo's blood tested, but Zully and Carlos have appealed. Gerardo is fourteen now, and the judge has asked him to appear in court. Who knows what he'll decide."

Gerardo, a broad-shouldered adolescent with chestnut hair and brown eyes, dressed formally in a three-piece suit, white shirt, and tie, sat in the judge's chambers between Zully and Carlos. When asked to express his wishes he did so unequivocally.

"I don't want to have a blood test."

"Even," the judge asked him, "if it helped to prove who your parents are?"

Gerardo looked from Zully to Carlos. "They are my parents. I don't want to know who my biological parents may be. They abandoned me."

"Perhaps not," the judge said. He nodded toward Sara and Mauricio. "If what these people say is true—"

"I don't care!" Gerardo said, not looking at them. "I belong where I am. I just want to be left alone."

"Please, Gerardo!" Mauricio said. "Simón! Look at us! We just want to know."

"You abandoned me! You had a baby knowing what could happen to people like you, and then you ran off to Spain and she—she confessed to being a terrorist and ended up in jail! Do you think I want to know that people like you are my parents?"

* * *

Mauricio had lived with guilt, regret, and endless soul searching for over a decade. Gerardo's refusal to even consider the possibility that he might be his son was the final blow. Three weeks after Gerardo's court appearance, Mauricio was in his workshop when the familiar pains assailed him. He managed to open the door and step outside. He had always said that he would die on the street, but he had thought his death would come differently, that he would die in a shootout like so many of his friends. Instead, he emerged into silence and solitude and caught a glimpse of a clear blue sky before he fell dead to the pavement.

CHAPTER IX

O, it is excellent
To have a giant's strength; but it is tyrannous
To use it like a giant.

WILLIAM SHAKESPEARE

E ster was at the hairdresser's when an Interpol agent appeared with a writ stating that she should present herself at the courthouse in San Isidro in Argentina within twenty-four hours. Miguel Angel Furci and his wife Elena González had finally been arrested and charged with the illegal possession of a minor.

A meeting had been arranged between Ester and Mariana, to take place in the judge's chambers.

Once more, Ester boarded the ferry, and presented herself at the courthouse. When the judge in charge of her case left the room, Ester had a few moments to compose herself before the door opened, and there standing in the doorway was a slender adolescent. Her eyes seemed a much darker blue than the clear, crystal gaze, like water in repose that Ester remembered. There was nothing restful or calm about the heavily made up young woman confronting her. Any hope she might have entertained that Mariana would rush into her arms and she could hold her as she longed to do, was dashed. It was clear that Mariana wished to be anywhere but where she was.

"Won't you come in and sit with me?" Ester asked her.

Mariana entered the room and chose a chair across from Ester and behind a low table.

"You know who I am, don't you?"

"You're the woman who had my parents arrested."

"I'd like you to know about your real parents, Mariana," Ester said.

"My name is Daniela."

Ester took out the photos she had brought. "This is your mother—Emilia. You'll see that you resemble her strongly! And this is your father—Jorge."

Ester put the photos on the table, facing Mariana, who glanced at them briefly.

"You know, Mariana," Ester said, "until today, I thought that you must be very strong. Now I think that more than strength what you've developed is armor."

"How would you defend yourself against all this? I wish you'd left us alone!"

"What if I had," Ester said, "and one day you discovered the truth about yourself? Wouldn't you wonder why your family hadn't tried to find you?"

"If you hadn't found me, I wouldn't have had to move to Paraguay! I hated it there! We lived like fugitives, under an assumed name. I had no friends. And now thanks to all the publicity you've stirred up I'm just a freak! I wish you'd given up looking for me!"

"Never!" Ester said.

"You didn't care how much you might hurt me?"

"I cared so much that I waited years for the courts to do their work. I see now that that was a mistake. I should have taken you that day when I saw you on your way to school!"

There was a soft knock at the door and a woman looked in.

"That's my grandmother," Mariana said. "I'm leaving now. We're going to visit my parents. In jail."

* * *

Violeta waited a long time for her friend to get off the ferry. Ester was among the last, and Violeta knew as soon as she saw her that the meeting had not gone well. Ester's face was drawn and her back stooped. Everything she had most feared had come to pass, she told Violeta. Mariana seemed not to want to understand what had befallen her.

"They say that forgetting is the dark side of memory," Ester said later, once Violeta had got her home. "That is what's happening to Mariana. She wants to forget all the dark things she remembers."

"She's spent her life in the care of people as different from Jorge and Emilia as one could imagine," Violeta said.

"Ironic, isn't it? Emi and Jorge devoted their lives to fighting everything the Furcis stand for, they died resisting the Furcis of the world, and their reward is to have their only child become a Furci."

With Mariana refusing to acknowledge her relationship to her biological family, all that remained to Ester was the hope of finding Emi's body, or at least of knowing where and how her last days had been spent.

* * *

Four days before Mariana's eighteenth birthday, Miguel Angel Furci was sentenced to seven years in prison. His wife, Elena González, received three.

One year later, Nino Gavazzo, whom Ester held responsible for taking Emi and Mariana to Orletti, and whom she believed was one of the last people to see her daughter alive, was charged with nothing more than extortion for trying to force a printer to make contraband Brazilian money. He was found guilty and sentenced to a few months of imprisonment.

Knowing that he was allowed to receive visitors, Ester went to see him. She was invited to wait, and shortly afterwards a lieutenant appeared and apologized in his name and the commander's for having kept her waiting.

"Are you a friend of his?" he asked.

"I wouldn't go that far," Ester replied and presented him with her card.

There was a long delay before the sweating lieutenant returned.

"*Señora*, what I need to tell you is that my commander cannot receive you now. It isn't that he doesn't wish to see you, he would like to chat with you, but this doesn't seem like the appropriate place. He would be pleased to see you at his home."

"I'll die of old age first!" Ester said. "Because if the justice system in this country ever does what it's supposed to do, he should be sentenced to life in prison. Tell him that what is really going on here is that he doesn't have the balls to face a mother trying to find out what happened to her daughter!"

Sara was waiting for her outside, and by the time Ester joined her, she was almost in tears. Rather than going home with the bitter taste of Gavazzo's cowardice in her mouth, she took Sara to the nearest café and treated them both to chocolate ice cream.

* * *

Sara too had continued her battle and not given up on Gerardo. She kept appealing Gerardo's decision not to submit to a blood test, until his case reached the Supreme Court. By then, Gerardo was of age, and his refusal to be tested was considered final, and put an end to litigation.

In 2000 Uruguay's new President, Jorge Luis Batlle, took office and created the *Comisión para la paz*—Peace Commission—

composed of six volunteers whose task it was to gather information. As one of them put it, "Our weapon is persuasion."

Working closely with a forensic team in Argentina, they managed to identify twenty of the estimated 140 Uruguayans who disappeared there.

Early in 2002, President Batlle chose to share with Sara a piece of confidential information confirming that Gerardo was not Simón, information which Sara discovered had been known by the government from the moment she and Mauricio instigated legal proceedings against Gerardo's adoptive parents.

"They knew?" Ester said furiously. "They knew from the start that Gerardo is not Simón?"

"It was all part of the pact of silence," Raúl said. "So long as we were on the wrong track, time was passing, the longer the better. Trails would grow colder, evidence would vanish, memories would grow dimmer, people would die."

Ester looked at Sara, sitting quietly by the open window. "How can you be so calm about it? I'd want to kill somebody!" Ester shouted. The pain she saw in Sara's eyes brought her to tears. "Oh, Sarita, I'm so sorry."

"I stopped searching," Sara said. "All this time, I stopped searching," she repeated, as if saying it again could make it not so. "And now here I am, back at the beginning after all these years."

The phone rang and Raúl picked it up. "It's for you," he said, handing the receiver to Sara. "Someone from the Peace Commission."

Sara took the phone and walked into the kitchen with it.

"Did Gerardo's parents Zully and Carlos know the truth?" Ester asked Raúl.

"They were kept as much in the dark as we were. But our government knew. It was part of the deal with the military. In the coverup they even lied to the Peace Commission."

They heard Sara's voice raised and stopped to listen.

"What proof have you got? I want to know! I have a right to know! If he's dead you have to prove it to me! Is there a body? I want to see it!"

Ester and Raúl ran into the kitchen.

"Who is it?" Raúl asked.

"The Peace Commission!" Sara said, throwing down the phone. "Simón is dead! He's dead!"

If Simón was dead then what had it all been for? He was the reason she had held on, through torture, through abandonment and betrayal. He had made it all meaningful. The river of pent-up grief she had damned during her twenty-six-year search was finally released, and Sara wept for the days spent at Orletti, for the years at Punta Rieles, for Carla and Emilia, for Simón, for Mauricio, and for herself.

Raúl and Ester tried to hold her, but Sara fought them off. She didn't want to be contained, to be comforted. No comfort was possible, no containment feasible. Her pain and grief were out of bounds, a force that would surely and mercifully kill her.

The cell phone in Raúl's pocket began to ring. He ignored it and tried again to hold Sara, who would have none of him.

"Answer it!" Ester said. "It could be important! Maybe she heard wrong! I'll take care of her!"

Keeping his eyes on Sara, Raúl moved back to the living room. "Hello! . . . Oh, hello, Margarita. No, it's not a good time . . . No, really, we've had some terrible news. No, please. Tell me later. I can't take it now. What?" He looked out the window and saw Margarita's car pulling up. He ended the call impatiently and went out to meet her. She had been there all the time, calling on her cellular phone.

"You have to listen," she told Raúl. "I have news of Simón."

"He's dead, we know!"

"Dead? Who told you that?"

"The Peace Commission just called Sara."

"Listen to me. I just returned from Buenos Aires, I came straight from the airport."

"Sara can't take another shock today!"

"She can take this one! Simón is alive! I've seen him!"

* * *

Sara sat as if turned to stone, her hands clasped in her lap and her eyes fixed on Margarita. Raúl and Ester sat on either side of her, watching her closely as Margarita asked them to cast their minds back to a night twenty-six years before when her father, Senator Zelmar Michelini, had been murdered in Buenos Aires. She and her brother Rafael had never given up on their efforts to bring their father's killers to justice. As soon as Rafael became a senator himself, he had access to more classified information and in the course of his investigations, he uncovered news about Simón. On the night that Sara and Margarita were taken to Orletti, Simón had been deposited at the doors of the Clínica Norte on Cabildo Street, where there was a nurse who distributed such children to families who wanted them. Rafael was given the names of three people who might have adopted Simón, and he was lucky on the first call— a police commissioner whose beat included the Clínica Norte. They spoke on the phone, and then met over coffee.

"Rafael says he will always remember the Commissioner stirring and stirring his coffee while he told him what happened on that coldest night of the year. A child had been left at the Clínica, which was in the Commissioner's jurisdiction, and he was notified. He was curious and went to see the child."

"Predator! Kidnapper!" Sara whispered.

"Commissioner Parodi was immediately drawn to the baby and his fluff of reddish hair."

A small cry escaped Sara, but she controlled herself at once and shook off Ester and Raúl's hands as if any touch would burn her.

"Parodi took Simón home where his wife fell in love with him. Rafael asked Parodi if the boy still lived with them. The man said he did and my brother asked him what made him so sure that he was Sara's son. Because, he said, only one child had been found that night. Rafael told Parodi that he would have to discuss all this with our president, but Parodi said nothing doing. The matter was between the two of them. I accompanied Rafael when we went to see the family."

"Was Simón there?"

"Yes. You will be proud of him Sara. He is a good man! But his family tree was cut down and another one planted all in a few hours," Margarita said.

Sara spoke at last. "So why did the Commission say he was dead? I don't understand." It was clear that she didn't want to be let down again.

"It's happened before. When disappeared children are close to being identified and found, the Commission's informants tell them they're dead. The Commission is as manipulated into its conclusions as every other group that has ever tried to find out the truth."

* * *

Sara had one day in which to grasp everything that had happened. In a daze, she dared not place too much hope in Margarita and her brother's assertions that this time Simón had really been found. She had been through too much to allow herself the luxury of any illusions. And then came the moment for which she had been preparing herself for nearly three decades. Simón telephoned her.

Sara had not concluded her mourning over the loss of that other child she had believed to be hers for so many years. And now here was another one. Sara realized that she had created a voice, a figure she wanted to find. One that resembled his father, his uncle, someone in the family . . . She was shocked when a totally different voice spoke to her.

For eleven days, while this stranger's blood was being matched with hers and with the sample Mauricio had deposited at the Durán Hospital in Buenos Aires, she attempted to lead her life as usual, but it was impossible to think of anything but the results. When she was assured that this was indeed Simón, for the first time in her life, Sara felt reluctant to act.

"I have to face a real image, not the one I've created," she told Raúl. "Let's not move too quickly until we're 100 percent certain."

Simón, who was 100 percent certain already, was impatient to meet his mother. His fiancée Emilce cautioned patience, but Simón couldn't wait and put together a photo album to send to Sara.

When Sara opened it she saw Simón learning to walk, Simón on the beach, Simón playing soccer. Simón, growing up without her.

The last photo in the book was of the baby she had left behind, sleeping in his green wicker basket.

EPILOGUE

June 2020

The damage of war has risen beyond all human right to wage it.

FREYA STARK

F rom the highest echelons of the Uruguayan government to the lowest, there was, at first, no official recognition that the disappeared existed.

In Sara's opinion, this hasn't changed. The government has made no commitment to finding the disappeared and the military's impunity has rarely been challenged. Twice, by popular vote, the military have been granted an armistice for their crimes.

Argentina took a different approach. With the return of democracy in 1983, investigations took place and military and civilian personnel involved in the disappearance and child trafficking of Argentine citizens and of Uruguayan residents, were held accountable. The divide that still exists in Argentina between those who justify what happened and those who condemn it is referred to as *la grieta*—the divide.

A National Commission on the Disappeared (CONADEP) was established, and as they openly admitted, "Seized by force against their will, the victims no longer existed as citizens. The authorities had no record of them; they were not being held in jail; justice was unaware of their existence. Silence was the only reply to all the *habeas corpus* writs, an ominous silence that engulfed them. No kidnapper was ever arrested, not a single detention center was ever located, there were no reports of those responsible being punished for any of the crimes. Days, weeks, months, years went by . . ."

As for the children who were taken during these arrests, the Commission reported that "Children who have witnessed the arrest of their parents in their own home . . . and the violent entry of armed groups, have suffered a traumatic experience, and this has naturally had a very serious effect on their personality." So serious, the report continues, that sometimes they died as a result. This was the case with Marcelo Barbagallo, whose house was broken into by an armed group who treated the boy roughly during the two hours they ransacked the house while they decided what to steal. He was forcefully separated from his mother and father when they were taken, and Marcelo was left in the care of his seventy-year-old grandmother. She told of how her grandson spent hours at the window waiting for his parents to return. They never did, and one morning in October of 1982 his grandmother found him dead. The cause of death was given as "a heart attack." Marcelo was twelve years old.

In spite of some government sponsored efforts, several Uruguayan children remain unaccounted for in Argentina, mainly those born to women who gave birth there.

Sara considers the harm done to disappeared children and their families to be irreparable. They have grown to love those who "adopted" them. When the truth is revealed to them, they discover that they have been living a lie, and that the people they have heard characterized as "terrorists" include their real parents.

As Sara's son told me, after he learned about Sara, he tried using the name Simón, but having spent more than 20 years using the one his adoptive family gave him—Aníbal—he couldn't get used to it. He wanted to blend both families, so he kept his first name and changed his last name to Sara's, becoming Aníbal Méndez.

Aníbal vividly remembers the evening Uruguayan Senator Rafael Michelini came to his house. The senator had already met with Commissioner Parodi, Aníbal's adopted father and had been invited to the Parodis home to break the news to Aníbal. Commissioner Parodi collapsed and wept. He had carried the secret of Aníbal's origins and of Sara's search for him for over two decades.

In shock, overcome with emotion, Aníbal asked for Sara's telephone number, and left the house. Arriving at his fiancée Emilce's home, he announced, "I am not their son."

Emilce was as shocked as he was. They had only heard people like Sara described as terrorists capable of anything and now Aníbal had announced that his parents were among them.

Holding the piece of paper on which Senator Michelini had written Sara's telephone number, and with Emilce by his side, Anibal telephoned her.

He is a man of few words, his speech measured, his voice gentle. Sara heard it for the first time when he said, "They say I'm your son."

Sara herself describes this moment as a good nightmare. She had faced disappointment so often that she couldn't accept Aníbal's proposal to meet at once. She would wait, she told him, until the DNA tests were complete.

Accompanied by members of the family that raised him, Aníbal went to the Hospital Durán, where both Sara and

Mauricio's DNA records were filed, and had his blood drawn.

The results were conclusive. No doubt remained that Aníbal was Sara and Mauricio's son.

Sara kept the news to herself. She did not want the media to hound Aníbal as they had hounded her on various occasions.

She tried to imagine how conflicted Aníbal must be. "Loving those he should reject," Sara says, "not only for having kidnapped him, but for separating him from his biological family, for giving him a false identity and a false history. As if that were not enough, these people taught him the ideology his parents opposed. In some cases, these same people were responsible for the death of an adopted child's parents. All this cannot but leave a deep imprint."

In spite of her reservations, as soon as the DNA results were confirmed, Sara could no longer postpone the moment. Aníbal traveled to Montevideo to meet his family. He knew that his father Mauricio had died, but discovered that he had two half-brothers, Mauricio's sons from his last marriage.

Aníbal remains determined to protect his adoptive parents and their two children, eight and ten years older than he. "They were also victims," he says. "They knew I wasn't their biological brother. They had been told to keep quiet." He finds it impossible to erase two decades of cherished family memories, and he struggles with feelings of ingratitude toward the family that raised him, loved and cared for him.

Sara refers to the Parodis as the "family that appropriated Simón." The Parodis refer to the Mothers of the Plaza de Mayo— among whom they include Sara—as "*las viejas locas*"—the crazy old women.

Deeply affected by what had been revealed about both families, Aníbal abandoned his studies—he had planned to join Commissioner Parodi in the police force—and left the Parodi's home to live with Emilce.

Eighteen months later, Commissioner Parodi died. Aníbal believes his death was the result of stress and the fear of being sent to prison.

While Aníbal went on to meet others like himself with whom he was able to share similar feelings of identity crisis, troubling questions surfaced along with conflicting emotions about families of origin and the families who raised them. Aníbal is alone in having a surviving biological parent—Sara.

He and Emilce married and now have a son, Juan Ignacio.

Sara's vision of the future is pessimistic. "I think this system, this order in which we live, is really a great disorder. I think it leads us to chaos and to the destruction of the world and of people, of all beings. The only thing we can do is struggle. If one does not resist, one becomes part of the world of the unjust, of those who oppress and subjugate others. We won't see the worst of it, our young people will."

I asked her what this worst could be. "The loss of values and ideals; the way money determines human relations and becomes the object of one's life. We may have erred on the side of being naive, we may have been short sighted, made poor choices, but we gave of our time, of our will, and even of our lives to bring about a more just world. Perhaps later we achieved government positions and failed to meet our goals, but our intentions, our vocation to service was real."

It saddens her that several of the friends who were imprisoned with her have children who ask them why they weren't considered during this struggle.

This belief that today's youth is incapable of understanding that the good of the community, of society as a whole, should prevail over the needs of the individual, is prevalent among parents and grandparents over fifty, who are seeing their society transformed into one where only material goods seem to matter.

* * *

Victoria remembers her childhood as pleasant. María Elena, the woman who raised her, was a widow. Her husband, Victoria's adoptive father, had been a police officer and had a powerful brother in the military. He died when Victoria was a year-and-a-half old, and his brother stepped in, keeping in close touch with Victoria and María Elena's son Juan. They lived in Belgrano, an upper-class area of Buenos Aires, and spent weekends at the country club. She describes the family as very supportive. Her adoptive mother María Elena did not get along with Juan, who was eight years older than Victoria, but had a very good relationship with Victoria herself, who became an intermediary between them.

Victoria knew she was adopted but suspected that something wasn't quite right. She first discussed her feelings with her first-grade teacher, who, given Victoria's age and what she shared about her adoption, decided to contact the Mothers of the Plaza de Mayo. Victoria's disappearance was already registered with them and they notified her grandmother Blanca in Montevideo. The wheels of justice turned slowly, but Blanca succeeded in bringing before a judge her decade-long search for her granddaughter, and her case to reclaim her.

Victoria was nine-years-old when her case was heard in court and she learned about her Uruguayan grandparents. All four grandparents—two from Uruguay, her mother Mary's country, and two from Argentina, her father Fredi's country—were there, and Victoria remembers feeling an immediate kinship with Blanca.

While the judge came to a decision, Victoria lived in Buenos Aires with a host family. Over the next three months the judge interviewed her and asked her what she wanted to do. Victoria opted on going to Uruguay, and the family came to get her. She remembers her grandmother Blanca fondly, but also recalls feeling very much alone. "They told me they were my family but I didn't know them. It was very hard moving to Uruguay. Everything was new and different, including school, where I had to learn all the history and geography of Uruguay."

However, it wasn't the learning that posed the greatest challenge. It was the change of social class. In Buenos Aires she had been a member of the upper middle class. In Montevideo she lived with her grandparents in the city's poorest neighborhood. She tried to adapt and make friends but the feeling of not belonging persisted. Blanca was a strong political and human rights activist, and Victoria met some of the friends who had been activists along with her parents. While at the time she did not feel a strong connection to their causes, she clearly took in their political ideals. She would go on to choose law as a career, specializing in human rights.

Both sets of grandparents understood Victoria's need to return to Buenos Aires often, not to see her adoptive mother as much as to meet with Juan, her adoptive brother. Victoria's Argentine grandparents made sure that Victoria visited them as much as possible, and when at age fifteen Victoria decided she no longer wanted to live in Montevideo they immediately came to take her back to Buenos Aires.

"The family in Uruguay," Victoria said, "was destroyed."

Back in Buenos Aires she sought out her brother Juan. When she told her paternal grandparents about Juan, she was told that she had to choose between Juan and them. Faced with this ultimatum, and unafraid of the court system, she personally appealed to the judge who had managed her case before, and he said he would speed up the process of her emancipation.

Victoria left her paternal grandparents house at once and began her law studies. She participated in demonstrations and in the work of the Mothers of the Plaza de Mayo. She had no income, so she found a part-time job a few blocks from her adoptive mother María Elena, who she had not seen for years. The judge, who had by now become a trusted friend and mentor, recommended that she talk to María Elena rather than risking an unexpected face-to-face encounter with her on the street one day.

Victoria took his advice, and she and María Elena resumed a relationship she described as "full of conflict." Victoria told Maria Elena that there were things she could never forgive, such as why she had agreed to adopt a child she must have known was not up for legal adoption. María Elena's answer—that her husband and his brother had assured her that the baby's parents were dead and no one had claimed her—only raised more questions. One thing was certain. María Elena loved and cared for her as a daughter, and Victoria admitted that what she felt for María Elena was something deeper than she felt for anyone else. In everything but blood, they were mother and daughter.

Following the Uruguayan tradition of taking both the mother's and the father's names, Victoria legally adopted the first name her biological parents had given her and her mother and father's last names. She is Maria Victoria Moyano Artigas.

* * *

Maria Ester's granddaughter Mariana speaks of her relationship with her Uruguayan family as being a "long process." When she learned about Ester and her search for her, she wanted none of it. She had no interest in her grandmother or anyone else in the family and only a vague memory of the incident when Ester saw her on the street and recognized her. She does remember Ester telling her that she and Mariana's paternal grandmother had waited at a certain distance, watching the front door of Mariana's house. Mariana went by them singing and when Ester said "what a pretty song" Mariana raised her eyes. That was when Ester recognized her.

The judicial process regarding her case began when Mariana was almost eighteen, and the Furcis—the couple who had raised her—had been tried and convicted for kidnapping and were in prison.

One of the first things investigators told her was that she had to meet her birth family. All she wanted, Mariana told me, was to get on with her life, preferably without them. But the family never gave up—"in a good way" Mariana added.

Their relationship began with telephone calls and letters, to which Mariana reluctantly responded.

In Argentina a person becomes of legal age at twenty-one, but just as in Victoria's case, the court saw the need to settle Mariana's case when it came before them. Mariana was almost eighteen and did not want to leave Buenos Aires. The judge respected that, giving guardianship to her adoptive maternal grandmother until Mariana came of legal age. The judge did stress, however, that Mariana had to try to establish a relationship with her Uruguayan family. Directives of this sort did not sit well with her. Mariana described her biological grandmother Ester as "a difficult woman with a very strong character." Ester lived alone and was dedicated to her principles and to the struggle to bring the military to justice.

Mariana felt a strong kinship with the Furcis and with her adoptive grandmother even after coming of age, when she left to live with her fiancé. Like Victoria, she graduated from law school, and shortly afterwards became pregnant. A traditional wedding was planned. It was important, Mariana said, that both families attend and that everyone behave well. They did. "Because they love me," Mariana said.

What Ester must have felt being in close proximity to the man who she had reason to believe had murdered her daughter Emilia and taken Jorge's place as Mariana's father can only be imagined.

When Mariana's daughter Agustina was born both grandparents came from Montevideo, along with two aunts. The reunion went well. Everyone was focused on the baby, and that, Mariana said, eased the pressure. Fortunately, they had not come to talk about Mariana's parents, because Mariana remained firm about not wanting to know. But the ice was broken and Mariana was more willing to accept them as family and not as "those people who come to tell me things."

When Agustina was two, she and Mariana were invited to her aunt's house in Uruguay. Ester and various cousins were there. "Ester was harder to get along with than the cousins," Mariana said. They agreed beforehand that the subject of her parents "and everything that had happened" would not be discussed. "I didn't want to know."

To this day Mariana speaks of the Furcis as "good parents. They raised me well and loved me very much. I love them. I didn't want the relationship to end."

Mariana tells me that her children—she has had two more since Agustina—"handle it all as if it were quite natural. They speak of 'the family here' and 'the family there.' They have no problems and are aware of everything."

* * *

Ester believed that it was during her effort to reconstruct Emi and Jorge's lives that she first understood "why disappearance is a permanent crime." Not only had she failed to find Emilia and Jorge's bodies, but Mariana refused to accept her. "It is not only the absence of mourning. It is a form of dying that doesn't allow for death or life. When I had a reason for fighting," she said, "it was as if my batteries were recharged after every encounter, and I could start each day with a new task. But now that it doesn't depend on me but on someone else, someone I love very much and with whom I suffer, because I know that Mariana is suffering, now I'm discouraged. Now I have nothing to fight for. No reason to fight. Part of what keeps me alive and vital is anger, rage. Every day the loneliness is worse, and I feel it more. I feel really alone. I am eighty-years-old and I think: how many years do I have left? Will they be enough?"

Years passed before Mariana had a change of heart, and through the network of the detained/disappeared she asked people who had known her parents to share their memories with her. She was warmly and enthusiastically received by them and welcomed into their network.

These years were especially difficult for Ester. They aged her prematurely and made her tired, but the photograph of Mariana finally standing by her grandmother's side during the annual *Marcha del silencio* (the Silent March) in Montevideo, show Ester smiling and radiant. The marchers demand that the search for the disappeared continue, and that trials and imprisonment for members of the military responsible follow suit.

Mrs. Furci has died, and her husband is in prison once again for crimes committed at Automotores Orletti.

* * *

Gabriel's parents, Carla and Fernando, were released from prison when Gabriel was four years old, and the couple sought exile in Belgium. A few months later Gabriel and his brother Daniel joined their parents there.

"That first year was very hard. We spoke no French and had to communicate with drawings. We lived with our mother and a friend of hers over a clock shop. The alarms went off all the time."

Exiled Argentines and Uruguayans often met in a house set up for their use, but Gabriel does not recall conversations about their pasts or the torture or imprisonment they had endured. His mother rarely mentioned it either.

"My mother is very hard inside. There must be a reason she doesn't want to talk."

Gabriel believes that some of the feelings that prevent her from talking are guilt over what happened to them, and jealousy of the relationship the boys have with the aunt and uncle who took them in when his parents were arrested.

The only times Carla made reference to her experiences in prison were times of stress. If the boys didn't want to eat the food she'd prepared, she would point out how grateful they should be for what they had, and describe the prison fare she'd had to eat, or food that was removed from her as punishment.

Gabriel knows that even though she rarely spoke of the past, it was not because she had forgotten it. It returned to haunt her at unexpected moments, like the time when Gabriel was a teenager and came home late from a party. He had forgotten his key, so he opened the gate by tapping it hard until it gave. His mother came out looking terrified. It was one of the few times she explained her reactions, or mentioned prison. The noise Gabriel made trying to open the gate had woken her, and for a moment she had believed herself back in her cell, where the guards often banged on the bars to startle the prisoners awake.

While his mother avoided talking of her prison experiences, she did explain to her sons the political activism that led to her being there. She did not ask them to forgive her, and they did not reproach her for actions that had placed them all in so much danger.

As for his father, Gabriel describes him as being "hermetically sealed" on the subject and unable to establish bonds of affection with his sons. They speak little; never of the past.

In 1995, when Gabriel was twenty-one years old and had finished his studies, he moved back to Uruguay to live with Antonio and Elena once again. His brother joined him, and with financial help provided by their father, they each bought a house.

He doesn't know what he would do if he found himself in similar circumstances to the ones his parents faced. He finds that impossible to predict, but he does feel strongly that he would not put his own children through the things he suffered.

In many ways, he hastens to add, he was lucky, and he knows it. His fate could easily have been that of his parents' friends the Juárez's, whose home was also broken into by Argentina's Special Forces when their son Sebastián was three-years-old. Just like Gabriel and his baby brother, Sebastián was left at a neighbor's house while his mother and father were hooded, handcuffed, and taken away. That neighbor too handed the child in her care over to the authorities—in Sebastián's case, the Minors' Court at Lomas de Zamora—where it was determined that he should go to the Casa de Belén Orphanage. Even though the judge was aware of the circumstances of his case, no investigations into his identity were carried out, and no photographs of him were published to aid the family in finding him. It took them seven years to locate him. Seven years during which Sebastián lived not knowing who he was or where he came from.

I tell Gabriel that cases like his and Sebastián's are one of my reasons for writing this book, and he nods. He would like to know why things happened as they did, how his family and the entire country came to be in such a pass. "I have a right to know," he says. "But my mother also has the right not to tell me. It would be good for our relationship if we could talk."

Knowing what I do about the circumstances of his mother's arrest and the interrogations she faced, I try to articulate how very difficult it is to talk about these experiences.

It is one of the ironies of being violated that it is the victim who feels the shame. It is even difficult, I tell him, for victims of torture to speak to mental health professionals. Fewer than 20 percent ever do.

He nods again, and our eyes meet. "I wish though," he says, "that politicians and people who lived through the events would hold seminars, make documentaries, explain how and why things happened as they did, and assure people that they will never happen again."

I tell him that the book I am writing is my contribution to that effort.

"Will people want to read about me and other children they don't know?"

"I hope they will," I say, and we agree that only time will tell whether it is possible to learn the lessons of war in a way that leads to peace, or whether war is so much a part of what makes us human that each generation must experience this deadly rite for itself.

Of all the issues Gabriel and Daniel have had to deal with, their aunt Elena identifies abandonment as the main one. She believes that they returned to Uruguay as young men to connect with their history. "I have a very strong memory of taking them for a walk through the old neighborhood, to see if they remembered any of it. When they went by the place where their nursery school used to be, they recognized it. 'We used to come here!' they said. 'We used to come here!' They wanted to see photos of themselves when they were little, because in Belgium they had had none. They looked through the photo albums, but asked for no details. I was surprised." She thinks that maybe the reason why they didn't ask what happened, how they were brought over to Uruguay, was either a lack of curiosity or simply a desire not to talk about such a painful subject. "Perhaps," Elena says, "they feel that they were not the most important things in their parents' lives."

Carla did not remarry and has had several partners, a situation her brother Antonio believes contributed to the boys' unstable adolescence.

They thank me for the opportunity my research has provided for them to revisit these events, because until now, just like Carla, "We didn't talk either! It was ingrained in us during the dictatorship."

"I have loads of friends, real friends," Antonio says, "who were imprisoned, and we've never stopped to talk, because I didn't ask, and they didn't want to tell me what it was like inside."

When Carla decided to join her sons in Uruguay, "I had to go to a psychologist to process her return," Elena says. "I would try to get close to her, but she would have none of it. I couldn't understand how she could treat me that way, when I had given her children their lives back. Antonio and I quarreled over it. Somehow, because Carla was his sister, I made Antonio responsible. There came a moment when we were getting along horribly. Again, again!"

Elena says that Carla's decision to join the guerrillas may have been heroic at the time, but it certainly came close to ruining her own life. "I was twenty-five years old, and I had to accept that whole situation. It destroyed a lot for us, including our relationship, which almost didn't survive. Antonio was studying, he had no time to see to my needs as a woman, or a mother, or anything. I was alone, absolutely alone. That rouses such anger in me! I can't speak calmly of those days."

Carla has never asked Elena about those years. "Never!" Elena says. She has come to accept that Carla may never touch the subject, perhaps due to feelings of guilt, of inadequacy as a mother. "It would be enough if she would only say 'thanks to you . . . ' It would be enough, but she can't do it."

"It would last our whole lives, that single moment of acknowledgement," Antonio says sadly.

"It would," Elena agrees.

* * *

The focus of my investigation has been disappeared children, but in the course of my research I have also spoken to military men active before and during the dictatorships.

Both the military and the former guerrillas who fought in Uruguay's civil war agree that it was the power seekers on each side who defined the struggle, and the idealists who paid for it.

What the victims request is that their suffering be acknowledged and remembered. That those guilty of the crimes of murder, kidnapping, torture, theft of property and of identity, face a just court empowered to hand out sentences commensurate with the crimes.

* * *

The September 11, 2001 attacks took place shortly after I began to write this book. Along with millions of others, I watched the horrors and the heroism that followed and wept, unable to escape an emotional premonition that somehow, the events I had so recently investigated were about to be repeated. As the weeks went by, I listened for voices like those I had so recently heard, voices that would encourage us to examine history and learn from it before applying old and failed strategies to this new situation. Underlying much of what I heard was incomprehension, puzzlement. Who could possibly hate us so much as to plan and execute such an attack? I knew that the answer to that question was complex and profound, but what I heard from our national leaders was that those who had attacked us "envied our freedoms." This shallow, sound bite analysis of the situation did little to further an understanding of how such envy could have inspired the depth of commitment to a deadly cause that led to the attacks. I became convinced that it was not freedom itself, but our interpretation of freedom, and what that interpretation has cost others, that engendered such rage against us.

As the weeks went by, I learned of the detentions without charges or legal representation, and of congressional approval for conducting secret military trials. I watched the attempt to carve up the world into friends and enemies, the effort to forge an international alliance to carry out the search for those enemies and to attack countries suspected of providing them with asylum. The more I heard, the more familiar the scenario became, until I plunged into a depression that made it difficult for me to distinguish between what was presently happening and the events I had so recently investigated.

When President George W. Bush announced that we were engaging in a war against terrorism, I was sitting in my study surrounded by copies of similar statements made by the South American military, who argued that if the guerrillas had a right to operate clandestinely and outside the law, so did they; and that they needed to redefine the rule of law in order to defend themselves and their countries. As the Patriot Act and the Military Order were approved, the feeling of reliving a nightmare became only too real. A few voices were raised in protest against the measures being suggested, but they were soon drowned out in the cacophony of calls for war and revenge.

When the authorities in Uruguay and Argentina first launched the initiatives they told us were essential for our safety and protection, we too disregarded the voices that warned against them. We were convinced that abuses and atrocities could never prevail in two such civilized nations. Our societies were based on a profound legal and social commitment to all citizens, and to women and children in particular. Among the best educated people in the world, we enjoyed a level of prosperity and comfort undreamt of by most of the so-called "developing" nations. Our faith in our systems, and in the people we had elected to oversee them, was so strong that we believed the systems themselves to be equally sturdy. Blinded to the limitations and the fragility of the intellects we had chosen to guard them, we were caught completely off guard by the horrors that followed.

By August of 1977, when Uruguay's military government gave itself the authority to arrest and try civilians with none of the legal safeguards provided by the constitution, we knew better, but by then it was too late.

On November 13, 2001, the United States Congress declared an "extraordinary emergency" and by means of the Presidential, or Military Order (Federal Regulation No. 57831) authorized the creation of special military tribunals to try non-citizens suspected of terrorism, leaving the decision of who will be brought before these tribunals entirely to the president.

In *Secret Trials and Executions,* Barbara Olshansky of the US Center for Constitutional Rights, explains that under the Military Order non-citizens "may be detained indefinitely without being charged or brought to trial; convictions and sentences by a military commission, including 'life imprisonment or death' can be reviewed only by the same officials who made the initial determination to charge the person accused: the president or the secretary of defense." They may also be tried in secret before a military panel on evidence that may not be examined or tested, convicted by a two-thirds vote, sentenced to death, and executed without Congress, the judiciary, or the American public ever knowing anything about any aspect of the proceedings. Thus, under President Bush's new Military Order, the checks and balances that define democracy are eliminated, public knowledge is censored, and the president, free from accountability, is invested with totalitarian power.

It is estimated that since 2001 the United States has held at least 30,000 people in this situation within its borders, and untold thousands more in sites outside the US.

"At the time the November 13 Military Order was signed, the United States Department of Justice had already detained more than 1,200 immigrants as part of its initial investigation," Olshansky writes, "and was in the process of authorizing local law enforcement agencies across the country to question 5,000 young men of Middle Eastern descent who had entered the country legally after January 1, 2000."

The Military Order, she continues, authorizes the secretary of defense "to determine the conditions of detention of the individuals who are charged under the Order. These provisions give the secretary license to detain individuals *indefinitely*. They also give the secretary the authority to specify the place of detention *anywhere in the world*.

"The USA Patriot Act requires that non-citizens who are detained by the government be charged with a crime or immigration violation within seven days of their detention. In contrast, no time limitations apply under the military order for informing those detained of the charges against them, nor do any avenues of judicial review exist for those being held. By means of the Military Order, then, the president has accomplished precisely those objectives which Congress would not accept when it considered the administration's proposal on the USA Patriot Act."

As explained in *Age of Anger*, by Pankaj Mishra, "The war on terror, aimed to abolish war as an institution with specific laws and rules, including regard for the rights of prisoners; criminalized the enemy and put him beyond the pale of humanity, exposed to extrajudicial execution, torture and the eternal limbo of Guantanamo."

In spite of, or perhaps because of, giving the president this unprecedented authority to act anywhere in the world, in the summer of 2002, when a new International Criminal Court (ICC) took jurisdiction in The Hague, ratified by sixty six nations, the United States was conspicuous for its absence. The Bush administration withdrew from the ICC, maintaining that no American should ever face trial in anything but a US court if accused of committing crimes during the exercise of his or her duties for the state. This in spite of the fact that anyone accused of a crime may first be tried in his own country's courts, and that the verdict will be accepted by the ICC.

When we recall that in July of 1999, 5,800 documents were declassified relating to the overthrow of the democracies of Latin America, and the crimes that followed, the reluctance to support an International Criminal Court becomes even more suspect. These documents implicate, among others, former President George H.W. Bush. Also former Secretary of State Henry Kissinger, who on June 20, 2001, returned to the Ritz Hotel in Paris to find the police waiting to serve him with a citation from Judge Roger LeLoire. He was being required to testify about the disappearance of five Frenchmen in Chile thirty years ago. Kissinger declined the judge's invitation and left Paris, making it impossible for him to return to France. A federal judge in Argentina has also submitted a judicial order asking for Kissinger's testimony. He has declined to appear.

When another 16,000 documents relating to the period 1976-1991 were declassified in November of 2000, Peter Kornbluh, of the National Security Archive, declared it "a triumph for the right of US citizens to know their own history."

That history includes US involvement in what winner of the 1980 Nobel Peace Prize, Adolfo Pérez Esquivel (in his foreward to Stella Calloni's book *Operación Condor: pacto criminal,*) called "an international terror"—the Condor Plan. It was under the provisions of the Condor Plan that many of the atrocities documented here were committed, as well as the assassinations of opponents of the military regimes, including Monsignor Oscar Romero, archbishop of San Salvador.

At the Nuremberg Trials which began in November of 1945 individual political and military leaders were for the first time held accountable by an international authority for atrocities committed in the name of a state. Benjamin B. Ferencz, who prosecuted members of the Nazi death squads at those trials, believes that in declining to participate in the International Criminal Court, the message given by the Bush administration was that "the United States is saying that we don't want the rule of law. I think that is dangerous, very dangerous, because we cannot lay down a law for the United States and not for the rest of the world. That doesn't fly. Law must apply to everyone equally or it's not law at all. Those who are pushing the other view have a misguided idea of what law is all about. They also have a misguided conception of how to safeguard the welfare and justice and rights for citizens everywhere."

* * *

While researching this book, I lost count of the number of times I heard and read various versions of the adage "Those who do not learn from their history are condemned to repeat it," and the passionately expressed hope that what happened in Uruguay and Argentina must be told and understood in order that no one need ever live through anything like it again. Even the book written by the Uruguayan *Junta* detailing its actions, begins with the quote *"Los pueblos que olvidan su pasado están condenados a revivirlo,"* which translates to: "Nations who forget their past are condemned to relive it." Yet among those who believe that, in the case of their own conduct at least, there is no benefit in looking back, none seem to want to believe it more strongly than the military themselves.

During the hours I spent with retired Colonel Ego Correa Luna, who generously shared personal experiences and documents with me, he often made mention of how much he wishes that people would put the events of the last few decades behind them.

When these events include the suspension of civil liberties that led to the disappearance of between ten to thirty thousand people whose absence serves as a daily reminder of the insanities unleashed by wars, looking forward remains fraught with difficulty for the people of Latin America.

Perhaps, when the past will not release us, it is because it isn't done with us yet, because we haven't learned the lessons it is trying so insistently to teach us. One of those lessons, I believe, is that every war is an effort to right the wrongs of the war that preceded it, trapping us in an endless cycle of violence.

POSTSCRIPT

In 2003 the glass memorial to Uruguay's disappeared was shattered by gunfire, but no matter how much some may wish them perpetually disappeared, every act of violence against them generates stronger remembrance.

* * *

On April 23, 2020, José Nino Gavazzo was found guilty of homicide, and of overseeing multiple disappearances. As the judge remarked, "It isn't necessary to have pressed the trigger to make you legally responsible for these crimes." Two months later, Gavazzo died of a cerebral hemorrhage. He holds the dubious distinction of being convicted for the largest number of murders in Uruguay's history.

* * *

In May 2021 the Inter-American Court of Human Rights heard the case of the Julien family's two disappeared children, Victoria and Anatole, who were kidnapped after the arrest and disappearance of their parents in Buenos Aires, Argentina, in September of 1976. The children were found abandoned in December of that year in Chile. They were adopted by a family there with no connection to the kidnapping and with no knowledge of who the children were. José Nino Gavazzo, under house arrest at the time, denied any knowledge of the case. Anatole, who was three years old when he was taken, remembered and recognized Gavazzo.

HISTORICAL
TIMELINE

1960	Daniel Mitrione assigned to US Office of Public Safety in Brazil.
1964	Uruguay breaks off diplomatic relations with Cuba.
1966	Military government established in Argentina
1969	Uruguayan Tupamaros set fire to the offices of General Motors in Montevideo.
1970	Elections held in Argentina.
	Salvador Allende elected president of Chile.
1971	General Hugo Banzer takes power in Bolivia.
	Four students killed at Kent State University in Ohio.
	Governor George Wallace shot in Alabama.
	Arab terrorists target the Olympic Games in Munich.
1970-72	Tupamaros kidnap several public figures, including British Ambassador Geoffrey Jackson.
1972	A state of internal warfare is declared in Uruguay.
1973	US topples Chilean President Salvador Allende's government.
	In Argentina the Montoneros hold nine foreign executives for ransom.
	A Ford Company representative is killed.
1974	Five military dictatorships now surround Argentina. Isabel Perón assumes the presidency.
	Operation Condor, a coalition between Brazil, Chile, Paraguay, Bolivia, Argentina, and Uruguay emerges. Juan Perón dies in July, having given foreign military intelligence services authority to arrest exiles in Argentina.
	Operation Condor's first high profile target, a former Chilean Defense Minister and his wife, are killed in a car bombing in Buenos Aires. Police and media report that the political left is responsible. Ten years pass before charges are brought against the political right.
	In Buenos Aires exiles form the *Partido de la Victoria del Pueblo.*
	Uruguayan children begin to disappear in Argentina.

Uruguayan Colonel Ramón Trabal, military attaché to England and France, is shot in Paris.

3,000 "subversives" are in jail in Uruguay

1975   Bernardo Leighton, leader of Chile's Christian Democratic Party and his wife are shot in Rome. Both survive.

Bolivian General Joaquín Zenteno Anayo is shot in Paris.

The Argentine Congress is dissolved and government buildings occupied by military personnel. The death penalty is established for political crimes.

General Jorge Rafael Videla declares this to be the first battle of the Third World War.

Venezuela and Colombia become the only democracies left in South America.

Uruguay, with a population of three million, is housing 7,000 political prisoners. Former Uruguayan Senator and Minister of Education Zelman Michelini and Héctor Gutiérrez Ruíz, President of Uruguay's House of Representatives are kidnapped and murdered along with two friends in Buenos Aires.

1977   The Mothers of the Plaza de Mayo begin weekly walks across from Argentina's Presidential Palace.

James Earl Carter, Jr. becomes President of the US.

1980   The Organization of American States releases a report stating that there can no longer be any question that torture was routinely practiced in Argentina and that thousands of disappeared persons had been murdered.

1981   Ronald Reagan defeats Jimmy Carter and the new Secretary of State, Alexander Haig, informs Argentina that it will receive no more public reproaches for human rights abuses.

1982   Argentina goes to war with Great Britain over the Falkland Islands.

1983   Elections held in Argentina.

1984   Elections held in Uruguay.

1985   Democracy is restored in Uruguay.

1986   In April, Argentina's National Commission on the Disappeared formally requests the extradition of three members of Uruguay's military forces.

1992   December 22, former chief of Chilean intelligence, General Manuel Contreras accuses the CIA (in whose pay he once was) of having ordered the murder of Carlos Prats and his wife in 1974, and of hiring a former CIA agent to do the job. Contreras also accuses former President George H.W. Bush of knowing this.

3,000 "subversives" are in jail in Uruguay.

1999	800 US documents declassified relating to the overthrow of democracies in Latin America.
2001	US Congress declares an "extraordinary emergency." Presidential or Military order authorizing the creation of special military tribunals.
	In Paris, Secretary of State Henry Kissinger receives a citation to testify about the disappearance of five Frenchmen in Chile.
2000	Uruguayan President Jorge Batlle creates the *Comisión para la paz*, a commission composed of six volunteers whose task it was to gather information and attempt to persuade the military to divulge the truth about the disappeared.
2002	International Criminal Court takes jurisdiction in The Hague. 16,000 US documents relating to the period 1976-1991 are declassified.

ACKNOWLEDGEMENTS

F irst and foremost heartfelt thanks to the mothers, grand-mothers, and relatives of disappeared children for their boundless generosity in sharing their stories and personal photographs. Also to the now adult disappeared children for their willingness to be interviewed and for their frank and open sharing of the experiences and emotions that have shaped their lives.

Maria Ester Francia made possible my introduction to the organization Mothers and Relatives of the Disappeared. The meetings that followed connected me to survivors of the dictatorship and to those relatives whose loved ones are still missing.

Lucía Todone assured those who wished to remain anonymous that I would honor their wishes, and hosted meetings at her home during which painful memories and events were relived.

Mariela Salaberry gave me access to the research she had conducted and to the book that resulted—*Mariana, tú y nosotros (Mariana, you and us)*. Without her generosity the extraordinary story of Maria Esther Gatti de Islas' decades-long search for her daughter, son-in-law and granddaughter, would have been difficult, if not impossible, to access.

My gratitude to retired Colonel Ego Correa Luna for sharing his impassioned defense of military actions and for giving me access to materials detailing and explaining military points of view and interventions.

Gustavo Camelot's willingness to update research, contact protagonists, and arrange long distance interviews was invaluable and made this publication possible. *Gracias* is too small a word.

Professor Roberto Gutiérrez Varea not only agreed to review the book before publication but provided corrections and perspectives for which I am deeply grateful.

Xandra Coe and Judy Meath deserve a special mention for their generosity and commitment to women in the arts. They gave unstintingly of their time and expertise to seeing that this book was published.

To the friends who supported what was often a difficult and challenging writing process, heartfelt thanks. Heidi Arneson read several versions of this manuscript and provided love and support at critical times during its creation. My appreciation and gratitude also go to Eloise Klein, Anne Welsbacher, Virginia Haggart, Renée Milstein, and Sylvia Crannell.

Without Minnesota's Invisible Ink Press's support, courage, expertise and invaluable editorial perspective, this book might have remained on the dark side of my memory.

Last, but no means least, my thanks to the staff of Books Fluent and Books Forward for the dedication and professionalism which made working with them a pleasure and a privilege.

9 781736 938607